W9-CST-366

791.43   **DATE DUE**

SEP 1 9 2006

DISCOVERING CAREERS FOR YOUR FUTURE

film

Ferguson

An imprint of ☑® Facts On File

Discovering Careers for Your Future: Film

Copyright © 2005 by Facts On File, Inc.

All rights reserved. No part of this book may be reproduced or utilized in any form or by any means, electronic or mechanical, including photocopying, recording, or by any information storage or retrieval systems, without permission in writing from the publisher. For information contact

Ferguson
An imprint of Facts On File, Inc.
132 West 31st Street
New York NY 10001

Discovering careers for your future. Film.
   p. cm.
Includes bibliographical references and index.
   ISBN 0-8160-5569-6 (hc : alk. paper)
 1. Motion pictures—Vocational guidance—Juvenile literature. I. Title: Film. II.
J.G. Ferguson Publishing Company.
  PN1995.9.P75D57 2005
  791.43'023'73—dc22   2004005340

Ferguson books are available at special discounts when purchased in bulk quantities for businesses, associations, institutions, or sales promotions. Please call our Special Sales Department in New York at (212) 967-8800 or (800) 322-8755.

You can find Ferguson on the World Wide Web at http://www.fergpubco.com

Text design by Mary Susan Ryan-Flynn

Printed in the United States of America

EB FOF 10 9 8 7 6 5 4 3 2 1

This book is printed on acid-free paper.

Contents

Introduction

You may not have decided yet what you want to be in the future. And you do not have to decide right away. However, you may already know that you are interested in film. Knowing your likes and dislikes is a great way to begin thinking about a career. Do any of the statements below describe you? If so, you may want to begin thinking about what a film career might mean for you.

___I enjoy performing in front of an audience.

___I like to make movies with my video or digital camera.

___I enjoy putting on plays with my friends.

___I like to use my hands to make or build things.

___I like to write songs, plays, or stories.

___I like to listen to or record sounds and music.

___I watch as many movies as I can.

___I play in the school band.

___I enjoy photography.

___I make my own clothes and jewelry.

___I spend a lot of time using art, illustration, or movie-editing programs on my computer.

___I enjoy drawing.

___I am fascinated by cartoons and the methods used to create them.

___I like to dance.

___I like to discover new music, movies, or books and tell my friends about them.

___I like to perform stunts with my bike.

Discovering Careers for Your Future: Film is a book about careers in film, from actors to film directors to screenwriters.

Careers in this field can be found on film sets, in recording studios, in business offices, in production houses, and in art studios. Although the film industry is centered in Los Angeles and New York, film workers are employed in most major cities in the United States and throughout the world.

This book describes many possibilities for future careers in film. Read through it and see how the different careers are connected. For example, if you are interested in working as a performer, you should read about actors, but also read about dancers and stunt performers. If you are interested in working behind the scenes in a creative position, you will want to read about cinematographers and directors of photography, costume designers, film directors, production designers, screenwriters, and other careers. If your interests are more technical in nature, you will want to read about audio recording engineers, lighting technicians, and special-effects technicians.

What Do Film Workers Do?

The first section of each chapter begins with a heading such as "What Film Editors Do" or "What Talent Agents and Scouts Do." This section explains what it's like to work at this job. It describes typical responsibilities and assignments. You will find out about working conditions. Which film workers are employed on film sets? Which ones work at computers in offices? This section answers these and other questions.

How Do I Become a Film Worker?

The section called "Education and Training" tells you what schooling you need for employment in each job—a high school diploma, training at a junior college, a college degree, or more. It also talks about on-the-job training that you can expect to receive after you are hired, and whether or not you must complete an apprenticeship program.

How Much Do Film Workers Earn?

The "Earnings" section gives salary figures for the job described in the chapter. These figures give you a general idea of how much money people with this job can make. Keep in mind that many people really earn more or less than the amounts given here. Actual salaries depend on many different things, such as the size and location of the company, the type of film project involved, and the amount of education, training, and experience the employee has. Generally, but not always, bigger film companies located in major cities pay more than smaller companies or independent film projects. People with more education, training, and experience earn more. Also remember that these figures are current salaries. They will probably be different by the time you are ready to enter the workforce.

What Is the Future of Film Careers?

The "Outlook" section discusses the employment outlook for the career: whether the total number of people employed in this career will increase or decrease in the coming years and whether jobs in this field will be easy or hard to find. The U.S. Department of Labor and this book use terms such as "faster than the average," "about as fast as the average," and "slower than the average" to describe job growth predicted by government data. These predictions are based on economic conditions, the size and makeup of the population, foreign competition, and new technology. Keep in mind that these predictions are general statements. No one knows for sure what the future will be like. Also remember that the employment outlook is a general statement about an industry and does not necessarily apply to everyone. A determined and talented person may be able to find a job in an industry or career with the worst kind of outlook. And a person without ambition and the proper training will find it difficult to find a job in even a booming industry or career field.

Where Can I Find More Information?

Each chapter concludes with a "For More Info" section. It lists resources that you can contact to find out more about the field and careers in the field. In this section you will find the names, addresses, phone numbers, and websites of film-oriented associations and organizations.

Extras

Every chapter has a few extras. There are photos that show film workers in action. There are sidebars and notes on ways to explore the field, fun facts, profiles of people in the field, and lists of websites and books that might be helpful. At the end of the book you will find a glossary, which gives brief definitions of words that relate to education, career training, or employment that you may be unfamiliar with. There is an index of all the job titles mentioned in the book, followed by "Browse and Learn More," which is a list of film books and websites.

It is not too soon to think about your future. We hope you discover several possible career choices in this book. Have fun exploring!

Actors

What Actors Do

Actors perform in stage plays, movies and television, video, and radio productions. They use voice, movement, and gestures to portray different characters. Actors spend a lot of time looking for available parts. They read and study the parts and then audition for the director and producers of the show. In film and television, actors must also do screen tests, which are scenes recorded on film. Once selected for a role, actors memorize their lines and rehearse with other cast members. Rehearsal times are usually longer for live theater performances than for film and television productions. If the production includes singing and dancing, it requires more rehearsal time.

Theater or stage actors may perform the same part many times a week for weeks, months, and sometimes years. *Film actors* may spend several weeks on one production, which often takes place on location—that is, in different parts of the

Screen Acting and Stage Acting

Screen acting differs from acting in a theater. In screen work, the camera can focus closely on an actor, so performances must be subtle and lifelike. Stage work requires more exaggerated gestures and speaking techniques. Film actors spend a lot of time waiting for scenes to be filmed. They repeat the same scene over and over, play scenes out of order, and perform only small segments of a scene at a time. Stage actors perform an entire play at one time. Screen actors do not know how audiences react to their performance until months after they finish work on a film. Stage actors get an immediate reaction from the audience while they are performing.

world. *Television actors* in a series, such as a soap opera or a situation comedy, also may play the same role for years, generally in 13-week cycles. For these actors, however, their lines change from week to week and even from day to day, and much time is spent rehearsing new lines. *Stage actors* perform an entire play, beginning to end, in one performance. Television and film actors usually perform scenes out of sequence during filming—they may perform the last scene first, for example. They also may have to repeat the same scene many times.

Acting is often seen as a glamorous profession, yet many actors work long and irregular hours for both rehearsals and performances, often at low wages. Actors must travel frequently to work in different theaters and on location.

Education and Training

Besides natural talent, actors need determination, a good memory, a fine speaking voice, and, if possible, the ability to sing and dance. Actors who appear in musicals usually have studied singing and dancing for years in addition to their training in drama.

Although it is not required, a college education is helpful for actors. High school and community theaters offer acting opportunities, and large cities such as New York, Chicago, and Los Angeles have public high schools for the performing arts. Special dramatic arts schools, located mainly in New York and Los Angeles, also offer training.

EXPLORING

○ Participate in school or community theater productions. You can audition for acting roles, but also work on costumes, props, or lighting to get theater experience.
○ See as many plays and movies as you can.
○ Read biographies of famous actors and other books about acting, auditioning, theater, and the film and television industries. You can also find biographies of actors on A&E Television Network's website at http://www.biography.com.

Study with the Masters

For over 50 years, The Actors Studio has taught the "method" style of acting to students. Method acting was developed from the work of Konstantin Stanislavsky of Russia and was taught by Lee Strasberg. It was made famous by Marlon Brando, Dustin Hoffman, Robert DeNiro, and many others.

The Actors Studio now has a master of fine arts degree program at the New School University in New York. The three-year program was created by studio members James Lipton, Paul Newman, Ellen Burstyn, Arthur Penn, Norman Mailer, Carlin Glynn, Lee Grant, and Peter Masterson.

The Actors Studio website is at http://www.new school.edu/academic/drama.

Earnings

The wage scale for actors and actresses is set by actors' unions. In 2002, the minimum daily salary of any member of the Screen Actors Guild (SAG) in a speaking role was $655, or $2,272 for a five-day workweek. Motion-picture actors may also receive additional payments, known as residuals, as part of their guaranteed salary. Many motion-picture actors receive residuals whenever films, TV shows, and TV commercials in which they appear are rerun, sold for TV exhibition, or put on DVD. Residuals often exceed the actors' original salary and account for about one-third of all actors' income.

The median yearly salary for all actors is $23,470. The lowest paid 10 percent earn less than $13,330 annually, while the highest paid 10 percent make more than $106,630.

In all areas of acting, well-known performers have salary rates above the minimums, and the salaries of a few of the top

FOR MORE INFO

This union represents television and radio performers, including actors, announcers, dancers, disc jockeys, newspersons, singers, specialty acts, sportscasters, and stuntpersons.

American Federation of Television and Radio Artists
260 Madison Avenue
New York, NY 10016
Tel: 212-532-0800
http://www.aftra.org

This union represents film and television performers. It has general information on actors, directors, and producers.

Screen Actors Guild
5757 Wilshire Boulevard
Los Angeles, CA 90036
Tel: 323-954-1600
http://www.sag.org

This site has information for beginners on acting and the acting business.

Acting Workshop On-Line
http://www.redbirdstudio.com/AWOL/acting2.html

stars are many times higher. Actors in television series may earn tens of thousands of dollars per week, while a few may earn as much as $1 million or more per week. In film, top stars may earn as much as $20 million per film, and, after receiving a percentage of the gross earned by the film, these stars can earn much more.

Outlook

Jobs in acting will grow faster than the average during the next decade, but acting is an overcrowded field. In the last two decades, the field has grown considerably outside New York because many major cities have started their own professional theater companies. The number of dinner theaters and summer stock companies has also increased. Cable television programming continues to add new acting opportunities, but there always will be many more actors than there are roles to play. Many actors also work as secretaries, waiters, taxi drivers, or in other jobs to earn extra income.

Audio Recording Engineers

What Audio Recording Engineers Do

Audio recording engineers operate and maintain sound equipment used during musical recordings, film production, and radio and television broadcasts. When monitoring the sound of a project, engineers use master console boards with many switches, dials, and meters. Sound levels must be read and adjusted during the recording process. As recording technology has advanced, the work of audio recording engineers has had a larger effect on the sound of the final recorded product.

Audio recording engineers who work in the motion picture industry supervise all sounds that are created during a film production. They test all microphones, chords, recording equipment, and amplifiers to ensure that actors' dialogue, sounds, special effects, and music are recorded correctly. They load tape players, set recording levels, and position microphones. Audio recording engineers often travel to film locations to set up and run sound equipment. They may work long hours on location and in the studio until a film is completed.

Audio recording engineers are assisted in the studio by *sound mixers*.

Websites to Visit

Broadcast Engineering
http://www.broadcastengineering.com

Mix Online
http://mixonline.com

Pro Sound News
http://www.prosoundnews.com

Remix
http://www.remixmag.com

These technicians monitor the sound quality of audio recordings. They use much of the same sound recording equipment and control panels to assist the audio recording engineer.

Audio recording engineers frequently perform maintenance and repair on their equipment. They must identify and solve common technical problems in the studio or on location.

Being a recording engineer requires both technical skills and communication skills. Engineers must be patient, be capable of working well with a variety of people, and possess the confidence to function in a leadership position. Excellent troubleshooting skills are essential for an audio recording engineer.

And the Oscar Goes To . . .

Here are some recent audio engineers who have won Academy Awards for their sound work.

Sound Mixing
2003: Christopher Boyes, Michael Semanick, Michael Hedges, and Hammond Peek for *The Lord of the Rings: The Return of the King*
2002: Michael Minkler, Dominick Tavella, and David Lee for *Chicago*
2001: Michael Minkler, Myron Nettinga, and Chris Munro for *Black Hawk Down*
2000: Scott Millan, Bob Beemer, and Ken Weston for *Gladiator*
1999: John Reitz, Gregg Rudloff, David Campbell, David Lee for *The Matrix*

Sound Editing
2003: Richard King for *Master and Commander: The Far Side of the World*
2002: Ethan Van der Ryn and Michael Hopkins for *The Lord of the Rings: The Two Towers*
2001: George Watters II and Christopher Boyes for *Pearl Harbor*
2000: Jon Johnson for *U-571*
1999: Dane A. Davis for *The Matrix*

Education and Training

During high school, take music courses to learn an instrument and learn music composition. You should also take classes in computer science and mathematics to prepare for the technical aspects of the career.

You will need a high school diploma and at least two years of further training at a community college or technical school to become a recording engineer. Those interested in becoming supervisors will need advanced degrees. While new engineers receive on-the-job training in station procedures, they are expected to know the basics of broadcast technology before they are hired.

Most engineers interested in breaking into the film industry begin their careers performing a variety of tasks for small film studios. As engineers gain experience and skill, they work up to more responsible positions and often move to larger studios or production companies. Some may eventually become supervisors or administrators, while others turn to teaching to advance their careers.

Earnings

Average earnings for audio recording engineers employed in the motion picture industry are approximately

An audio recording engineer adjusts controls during a recording session. (Photo Disc)

EXPLORING

○ If your school has a media department, learn how to work with some of the basic equipment.

○ Join a music or theater club to work in a sound booth during a live production.

○ Write or call record companies, recording studios, or motion picture studios to get more information.

○ Read books and music trade magazines that cover sound production.

FOR MORE INFO

For information on audio recording schools and courses, contact
Audio Engineering Society
60 East 42nd Street, Room 2520
New York, NY 10165
Tel: 212-661-8528
http://www.aes.org

For facts and statistics about the recording industry, contact
Recording Industry Association of America
1330 Connecticut Avenue, NW, Suite 300
Washington, DC 20036
Tel: 202-775-0101
http://www.riaa.com

For general information, contact
Society of Professional Audio Recording Services
PO Box 770845
Memphis, TN 38177
Tel: 800-771-7727
http://www.spars.com

$60,600. Audio recording engineers employed in all industries have earnings that range from less than $18,540 to $82,510 or more annually.

Outlook

Employment in this field is expected to grow at an average rate. Computer technology will continue to make the recording process easier, which may limit some jobs for entry-level studio technicians. However, as the film industry grows and the recording process becomes faster, more audio recording engineers will be needed. Engineers with an understanding of advanced technologies, such as digital recording and multimedia, will have an edge over the competition.

Camera Operators

What Camera Operators Do

Camera operators use motion picture cameras and equipment to photograph subjects for movies, television programs, or commercials. Camera operators may work on feature films in Hollywood or on location elsewhere. Many work on educational films, documentaries, or television programs. The nature of the camera operator's work depends largely on the size of the production crew. If the film is a documentary or short news segment, the camera operator may be responsible for setting up the camera and lighting equipment and supervising the actors during filming. Equipment that camera operators typically use includes cranes, dollies, mounting heads, and different types of lenses and accessories. Often the camera operator is also responsible for maintenance and repair of all of this equipment.

With a larger crew, the camera operator is responsible only for the actual filming. The camera operator may even have a support team of assistants. The *first assistant camera operator* will typically focus on the cameras, making sure they are loaded and operating correctly. In larger productions, there are also backup cameras and accessories for use if one should malfunction during filming. *Second assistant camera operators* help the first assistant set up scenes to be filmed and assist in the maintenance of the equipment.

Read All about It

Learn about the film industry by reading these publications:

American Cinematographer
http://www.theasc.com/magazine

Cinefex
http://www.cinefex.com

EXPLORING

○ Join a photography or camera club, or become involved with the media department of your school. You may have the opportunity to videotape sports events, concerts, and school plays.

○ Offer to work part time or volunteer at a camera shop. This will give you a basic understanding of photographic equipment.

○ If your school has a television station, see if you can learn the basics of camera operation.

Sometimes camera operators must use shoulder-held cameras. This often occurs during the filming of action scenes for television or motion pictures. *Special effects camera operators* photograph the optical effects segments for motion pictures and television. They create visual illusions that can add mood and tone to a motion picture.

Education and Training

In high school, take classes in photography, journalism, and media arts. Mathematics and science can help you in understanding cameras and filters. You should also take art and art history classes and other courses that will help you appreciate visual styles.

A college degree is not necessary to get a position as a motion picture camera operator, but attending film school can

Top Camera Work

In 2003, the late cinematographer Conrad L. Hall was awarded an Outstanding Achievement Award by the American Society of Cinematographers (ASC) for his work on the film *Road to Perdition*. It was the fourth time that Hall has taken top honors in the annual ASC competition. He previously won for *Tequila Sunrise* (1989), *Searching for Bobby Fischer* (1994), and *American Beauty* (2000). Hall died on January 4, 2003. The award was accepted on his behalf by his son Conrad W. Hall.

help you expand your network of connections. A bachelor's degree in liberal arts or film studies provides a good background for work in the film industry. However, practical experience and industry connections will provide the best opportunities for work.

Earnings

Salaries vary widely for camera operators. The median annual earnings of all television, video, and movie camera operators is $32,720. The lowest paid 10 percent of operators earn less than $14,710 per year, and the highest earning 10 percent make more than $65,070 annually.

FOR MORE INFO

For lists of tricks of the trade and favorite films of famous cinematographers, visit the ASC website.
American Society of Cinematographers (ASC)
PO Box 2230
Hollywood, CA 90078
Tel: 800-448-0145
http://www.theasc.com

For information on membership benefits, contact this branch of the International Alliance of Theatrical Stage Employees (IATSE).
International Cinematographers Guild (IATSE Local 600)
National Office/Western Region
7755 Sunset Boulevard, Suite 300
Hollywood, CA 90046

Tel: 323-876-0160
http://www.cameraguild.com

To learn about student chapters sponsored by the SMPTE, contact
Society of Motion Picture and Television Engineers (SMPTE)
595 West Hartsdale Avenue
White Plains, NY 10607
Tel: 914-761-1100
http://www.smpte.org

Visit this website organized by the ASC for a list of film schools and to learn about the career of cinematographer—the next step on the career ladder for camera operators.
Cinematographer.com
http://www.uemedia.com/CPC/cinematographer

Outlook

Employment for camera operators is expected to increase faster than the average for all occupations in the coming years. The use of visual images continues to grow in areas such as education, entertainment, marketing, and research and development. More businesses will make use of video training films and public relations projects that involve film. The entertainment industries are also expanding. However, competition for positions will remain very fierce. Camera operators work in what is considered a desirable and exciting field, and they must work hard and be aggressive to get good jobs, especially in Los Angeles and New York.

Cartoonists and Animators

What Cartoonists and Animators Do

Animators, often called *motion cartoonists,* design the cartoons you see on television and at the movies. They also create the digital effects for many films and commercials. Computer animators created more than 2,000 of the effects in *Star Wars: Episode I—The Phantom Menace.* Making a big animated film, such as *A Bug's Life* or *Shrek,* requires a team of many creative people. Each animator on the team works on one small part of the film. On a small production, animators may be involved in many different aspects of the project's development.

An animated film begins with a script. *Screenwriters* plan the story line, or plot, and write it with dialogue and narration. *Designers* read the script and decide how the film should look—should it be realistic, futuristic, or humorous? They then draw some of the characters and backgrounds. These designs are then passed on to a *storyboard artist* who illustrates the whole film in a series of frames, similar to a very long

Animation on the Web

You can find lots of animation information on the Internet. Try these websites:

Animation Artist (http://www.animationartist.com)

Animation Magazine (http://www.animationmagazine.net)

Animation USA (http://www.animationusa.com/index.html)

Kaleidoscapes Cool Kids' Animation (http://www.kaleidoscapes.com/current.html)

Pixar (http://www.pixar.com)

StopMotionAnimation.com (http://www.stopmotionanimation.com)

comic strip. Based on this storyboard, an artist can then create a detailed layout.

The most common form of animation is *cell animation*. Animators examine the script, the storyboard, and the layout, and begin to prepare the finished artwork frame by frame, or cell by cell, on a combination of paper and transparent plastic sheets. Some animators create the "key" drawings—these are the drawings that capture the characters' main expressions and gestures at important parts in the plot. Other animators create the "in between" drawings—the drawings that fill in the spaces between one key drawing and the next. The thousands of final black and white cells are then scanned into a computer. (A television cartoon has 25–30 images per second.) With computer programs, animators add color, special effects, and other details.

In *stop-motion animation*, an object such as a clay creature or doll is photographed, moved slightly, and photographed again. The process is repeated hundreds of thousands of times. Movies such as *Chicken Run* were animated this way. In computer or digital animation, the animator creates all the images directly on the computer screen. Computer programs can create effects like shadows, reflections, distortions, and dissolves.

Education and Training

Art and drawing classes will prepare you for a career in animation. Photography classes can help you to develop visual composition skills.

EXPLORING

- Practice sketching. Carry a sketchpad around in order to quickly capture images and gestures that seem interesting to you.
- There are many computer animation software programs that teach basic principles and techniques. Experiment with these programs to create basic animation.
- Participate in school or community art clubs. Draw posters to publicize sporting events, dances, and meetings.
- Some video cameras have stop-motion buttons that allow you to take a series of still shots. You can use this feature to experiment with claymation and other stop-motion techniques.

Words to Learn

animatic kind of digital storyboard that allows animations to be viewed on a video monitor

fps frames per second; in general, the higher the number of frames, the better the animation will be

kinematics animating a model to move the way a human moves

layers used in complex animation to help manipulate objects; different objects can be assigned different layers and then moved independently

modeling process used to make animated objects from a real object; animators use models to help them envision the object and figure out how to draw its movements on flat paper

rendering making a character or an inanimate object seem lifelike; artists use color, shadow, texture, and light to render

storyboarding an outline of an animation in a series of drawings in multiple frames

English composition and literature classes will help you develop creative writing skills. Computer classes are important for learning to use art-related software, such as illustration, graphics, and animation programs.

A college education is not required for this career, but there are a number of animation programs offered at universities and art institutes across the country. You may choose to pursue a bachelor's, a master's of fine art, or a Ph.D. in computer animation, digital art, graphic design, or art. Some of today's top computer animators are self-taught or have learned their skills on the job.

Earnings

According to *U.S. News & World Report,* animators, depending on their experience, can earn from $800 to $1,800 a week. Top

FOR MORE INFO

For information about animated films and digital effects, visit the AWN website, which includes feature articles, a list of schools, and a career section.

Animation World Network (AWN)
6525 Sunset Boulevard, Garden Suite 10
Hollywood, CA 90028
Tel: 323-606-4200
http://www.awn.com

For festival listings and information on animation preservation, visit the IAFS website.

International Animated Film Society (IAFS)
721 South Victory Boulevard
Burbank, CA 91502
Tel: 818-842-8330
http://www.asifa-hollywood.org

For an overview of animation and useful exercises, visit the following website:
Animating: Creating Movement Frame by Frame
http://www.oscars.org/teachersguide/animation/download.htm

animators can command weekly fees of about $6,500 or more. Salaried animators had average earnings of $43,980 in 2003, according to the U.S. Department of Labor. The lowest paid 10 percent earned $25,830 or less, and the highest paid 10 percent earned $85,160 or more annually. Very experienced and successful animators, designers, and art directors can earn over $1 million a year.

Outlook

Opportunities in this field are expected to grow faster than average, according to the U.S. Department of Labor. Animated films continue to make millions of dollars at the box office. Cable television is also producing more and more successful animated series for both children and adults. No matter how many animation projects there are, however, it will likely remain very difficult to get a job at a studio. Pixar, the studio that created *Monster's, Inc.* and *Finding Nemo*, receives about 2,000 reels (short films demonstrating the work of animators) a year from hopeful job candidates. Of this number, the studio will hire fewer than 100 animators.

Cinematographers and Directors of Photography

What Cinematographers Do

Cinematographers, also known as *directors of photography*, run the cameras during the making of a film or video. They work closely with directors, actors, and members of the film crew. Cinematographers work on feature films, educational films, industrial training films, documentaries, and commercials. Specific job duties depend on the size of the production. For a documentary with a small crew, a cinematographer may set up the lighting and camera equipment and direct the movements of the actors. For a larger production, the cinematographer might concentrate solely on running the camera, while a team of assistants helps out with loading and unloading film and setting up the equipment.

Cinematographers begin work on a film project by reading the script. They discuss with the director how to film each scene. They decide whether to film from across the room, or up close to the actors. They decide whether to use bright lighting with lots of shadows or more muted, even lighting. They decide on camera angles, how the camera moves, and how to frame each scene. Cinematographers also have a great deal of technical knowledge about film, which helps them

Check It Out

Go to your local video store and rent the documentary *Visions of Light* (1992), directed by Arnold Glassman and Todd McCarthy. This movie provides an introduction to some of the finest cinematography in the history of film.

Cinematographers must have a keen eye for detail as they set up cameras and other equipment. (Photo Disc)

decide which cameras, film, and filters to use. Cinematographers are also in charge of the film crew. They hire various assistants and give them detailed instructions on how to film each scene.

Cinematographers work both indoors and outdoors. They sometimes spend several months on location away from home. When working on smaller productions, there may be a limited budget and a smaller film crew, so cinematographers may have to load and unload film from the camera, set up tripods, and carry cameras long distances. They participate in long hours of rehearsal before they actually start to film a scene. Although all their work is behind the scenes, cinematographers play an important part in the appearance and the success of the final film.

It's a Fact

In 1928, the first Oscars awarded in the category of cinematography went to Charles Rosher and Karl Struss for *Sunrise*.

In 1939, the Academy of Motion Picture Arts and Sciences began to give separate awards for black-and-white and color cinematography. That year, Gregg Toland won in the black-and-white category for *Wuthering Heights* and Ernest Haller and Ray Rennahan won in the color category for *Gone with the Wind*.

In 1966, the last award for black-and-white cinematography was awarded to Haskell Wexler for *Who's Afraid of Virginia Woolf?*

Only one cinematographer has won four Oscars: Leon Shamroy for *The Black Swan* (1942), *Wilson* (1944), *Leave Her to Heaven* (1945), and *Cleopatra* (1963).

Education and Training

Art and photography courses can help you understand the basics of lighting and composition. When you get to high school, take broadcast journalism or media courses that teach camera operation and video production.

A college degree is not always necessary to find a position as a cinematographer. Experience is much more important. Many cinematographers, though, get this valuable experience during their college studies. Many colleges and art schools offer programs in film or cinematography.

Your training should include all aspects of camera operations and lighting. It is important to practice working on a team. You must be able to give directions as well as follow them.

Earnings

When starting out, apprentice filmmakers may make no money. They may even spend their own money to finance their own projects. Since they usually are hired one film at a time, there may be periods where they do not receive pay between assignments. As a cinematographer gains experience, he or she will begin to find more jobs and earn more. Well-established cinematographers working on big-budget productions can make well over $1 million a year, but very few cinematographers earn that much. For union members, the minimum pay is $523 a day for a feature film. For location shoots, the wage is $671 a day.

EXPLORING

○ Watch as many movies as you can. Study them closely for the styles of the filmmakers.

○ If you have access to a 16-mm camera, a camcorder, or a digital camera, you can experiment with composition, lighting, and other skills.

○ Check with your school's media center or journalism department about recording school events on film.

○ Your school's drama club may offer opportunities to work on writing and staging your own productions.

○ Read magazines such as *American Cinematographer, Daily Variety, Hollywood Reporter,* and *Cinefex* to learn more about filmmaking.

FOR MORE INFO

For information about colleges with film and television programs of study and to read interviews with filmmakers, visit the AFI website.

American Film Institute (AFI)
2021 North Western Avenue
Los Angeles, CA 90027
Tel: 323-856-7600
http://www.afi.com

This website has articles from American Cinematographer *magazine, industry news, and a students' section with grants and fellowship information.*

American Society of Cinematographers (ASC)
PO Box 2230
Hollywood, CA 90036
Tel: 800-448-0145
http://www.theasc.com

For an overview of cinematography and useful exercises, visit the following website:

Cinematography: Capturing Images on Film
http://www.oscars.org/teachersguide/
cinematography/download.html

Outlook

Employment for camera operators should grow faster than the average in coming years. However, there are far more qualified cinematographers than there are job openings. If you are skilled and well trained, you should find positions, but it could take a long time before you find work in Los Angeles or New York.

You may find better opportunities working on TV commercials, documentaries, or educational films. Cinematographers of the future will be working closely with special effects experts. Computer technology can create crowd scenes, underwater images, and other effects more easily and cheaply. Cinematographers will have to approach a film with an understanding of which shots can be made digitally and which shots will need traditional methods of filmmaking.

Composers

What Composers Do

Composers write music for musical stage shows, television commercials, movies, ballet and opera companies, orchestras, pop and rock bands, jazz combos, and other musical performing groups. Composers work in many different ways. Often they begin with a musical idea and write it down using standard music notation. They use their music training and their own personal sense of melody, harmony, rhythm, and structure. Some compose music as they play an instrument and may or may not write it down.

Most composers specialize in one style of music, such as classical, jazz, country, rock, or blues. Some combine several styles. Composers who work on commission or on assignment meet with their clients to discuss the composition's theme, length, style, and the number and types of performers. Composers work at home, in offices, or in music studios. Some need to work alone to plan and build their musical ideas and others work with fellow musicians. Composing can take many long hours of work, and composing jobs may be irregular and low paying. However, it is extremely satisfying for composers to hear their music performed, and successful commercial music composers can

Words to Learn

Composers use the following words to tell musicians how fast or slow to play:

largo   slow and noble

adagio   not as slow as largo

lento   slow; between adagio and andante

andante   moderately slow

moderato   moderate

allegretto   moderately fast

allegro   fast

vivace   lively

presto   very fast

EXPLORING

- ○ Participate in musical programs offered by local schools, YMCA/YWCAs, and community centers.
- ○ Learn to play a musical instrument, such as the piano, guitar, violin, or cello.
- ○ Watch movies and listen to their musical scores
- ○ Attend concerts and recitals.
- ○ Read about composers and their careers.
- ○ Form or join a musical group and try to write music for your group to perform.

earn a lot of money. After the piece is completed, the composer usually attends rehearsals and works with the performers. The composer may have to revise parts of the piece until the client and the composer are satisfied.

Many composers never perform their own works, but others, especially pop, rock, jazz, country, or blues performers, compose music for their own bands to play.

Education and Training

All composers need to have a good ear and be able to notate, or write down, their music. Composers of musicals, symphonies, and other large works must have years of study in a college, conservatory, or other school of music. Composers of popular songs may not need as much training. However, studying music helps you develop and express your musical ideas better. Music school courses for those who wish to be composers include music theory, musical form, music history, composition, conducting, and arranging. Composers also play at least one musical instrument, usually piano, and some play several instruments.

Earnings

Most composers earn very little and work only part time, while a few earn a great deal. Some composers work on commission. When a piece of music is commissioned, the composer receives a lump sum for writing it. Other composers work under contract with a music publishing, recording, or motion-picture company. Their compositions become the

More Words to Learn

Composers use the following words and abbreviations to tell musicians how loud or soft to play:

pianissimo (pp)   very soft

piano (p)   soft

mezzopiano (mp)   half-soft

**diminuendo or descrescendo
(dim; decresc. or >)**   growing softer

mezzoforte (mf)   half loud

forte (f)   loud

fortissimo (ff)   very loud

crescendo (cres. or <)   growing louder

fortepiano (fp)   loud, then soft

sforzando or sforzato (sf; sfz) sudden, strong accent

property of the company. Some composers receive royalties, or payments for each performance or sale of the piece.

A major film studio may pay a composer $50,000 to $200,000 or more for a musical score. A composer may be paid per episode for a television program or series, ranging from $1,000 to $8,000.

For music written for the theater, pay is based on the size and type of the theater company or play. Composers for the theater earn from $3,000 to $12,000 per show. A small opera company may pay in the range of $10,000 to $70,000. Large opera companies pay from $15,000 to $150,000.

Outlook

The U.S. Department of Labor, which classifies composers and arrangers in the category of musicians, singers, and related workers, predicts employment in this field to grow about at an average rate during the next decade. As long as there are movies, commercials, musicals, operas, orchestras, and musical performers, there will be a need for composers to write music.

FOR MORE INFO

For profiles of composers of concert music, visit the ACA website.
American Composers Alliance (ACA)
73 Spring Street, Room 505
New York, NY 10012
Tel: 212-362-8900
http://www.composers.com

For music news, news on legislation affecting musicians, and the magazine International Musician, *contact*
American Federation of Musicians
1501 Broadway, Suite 600
New York, NY 10036
Tel: 212-869-1330
http://www.afm.org

For articles on songwriting, information on workshops and awards, and practical information about the business of music, contact
American Society of Composers, Authors and Publishers
One Lincoln Plaza
New York, NY 10023
Tel: 212-621-6000
http://www.ascap.com

Costume Designers

What Costume Designers Do

Costume designers create the costumes seen in the theater, on television, and in the movies. They also design costumes for figure skaters, ballroom dancers, and other performers. During the planning of a show, costume designers read the script. They meet with directors to decide what types of costumes each character should wear for each scene.

Stories that take place in the past, called period pieces, require costume designers to have a great deal of knowledge about what people wore during different historical time periods in different parts of the world. Designers do research at libraries, museums, and universities to study the garments, shoes, hats, belts, bags, and jewelry worn by men, women, and children. They look at the colors and types of fabric used and how garments were made. Even for stories that take place in modern times or in the future, costume designers might use ideas that come from looking at the details of historical fashions.

Starting at the Bottom

One of ancient people's first articles of clothing was protective covering for the feet. Animal hides were ideal for the purpose. In warm climates the typical footwear was the sandal, a sole with straps to hold it on. In colder climates, people wore shoes that wrapped around the foot and sometimes extended into boots. In ancient Greece and Rome the soles of soldiers' sandals were studded with hobnails, or large-headed nails, for longer wear. Armies continued to use hobnail boots into modern times.

A costume designer prepares new sketches for an upcoming film. These sketches must meet the director's approval before work on the actual costumes can begin. (NYS Theatre Institute)

Once the research is finished, designers begin to make sketches of their costume ideas. They try to design each outfit to look authentic, or true to the time period when the story occurs. Designers also pay attention to the social status of each character, the season and weather for each scene, and the costumes of other characters in each scene.

Costume designers meet with directors for design approval. They also meet with stage designers or art directors to be certain that the furniture and backdrops do not clash with the costumes. They meet with lighting designers to make sure that the lighting will not change the appearance of costume colors.

Costume designers decide whether to rent, purchase, or sew the costumes. They shop for clothing and accessories, fab-

Don't Forget the Accessories

Costumes include a lot more than clothing. Designers have to also consider accessories, such as the following:

○ belts and girdles, including sword belts, sashes, and suspenders
○ neckwear, such as ruffs, collars, cravats, neckties, and tie clasps
○ eyeglasses, including monocles, lorgnettes, and pince-nez

○ fans
○ jewelry, including earrings, pins, necklaces, beads, bracelets, rings, and watches
○ gloves
○ purses and pouches
○ shawls
○ umbrellas and parasols
○ walking sticks and canes

rics, and sewing supplies. They also supervise assistants who do the sewing.

Education and Training

To become a costume designer, you need a high school education and a college degree in costume design, fashion design, or fiber art. You also need experience working in theater or film.

English and literature courses will help you read and understand scripts. History classes are helpful for researching historical costumes and time periods. Courses in sewing, art, designing, and draping are also necessary.

Earnings

For feature films and television, costume designers earn daily rates for an eight-hour day or a weekly rate for an unlimited number of hours. Costume designers who work on Broadway or for dance companies in New York City are usually members of United Scenic Artists union, which sets minimum rates for its members. A costume designer for a Broadway musical with a minimum of 36 actors earns around $17,500. For opera and dance companies, salary is usually by costume count. Designers sometimes earn royalties on their designs.

Most costume designers work freelance and are paid per costume or show. Costume designers can charge between $90 and $500 per costume, but some costumes, such as those for figure skaters, can cost thousands of dollars.

EXPLORING

○ Join a school drama club or a community theater. Volunteer to work on costumes or props. School dance troupes or film classes also offer opportunities to explore costume design.
○ Learn to sew. Once you are comfortable sewing clothes from commercial patterns you can begin to make some of your original designs.
○ *The Costumer's Handbook* and *The Costume Designer's Handbook,* both by Rosemary Ingham and Elizabeth Covey, are good resources for beginning or experienced costume designers.
○ Practice designing costumes on your own. Draw sketches and try to imitate designs you see on television, in films, or on the stage.

FOR MORE INFO

This union represents costume designers in film and television. For information on the industry and to view costume sketches in their online gallery, visit the Guild's website.

Costume Designers Guild
4730 Woodman Avenue, #430
Sherman Oaks, CA 91423
Tel: 818-905-1557
http://www.costumedesignersguild.com

This organization provides a list of costume design schools.

The Costume Society of America
PO Box 73
Earleville, MD 21919
Tel: 800-272-9447
Email: national.office@costumesociety
america.com
http://www.costumesocietyamerica.com

Outlook

Competition among costume designers is stiff and will remain so throughout the next decade. There are many more qualified costume designers than there are jobs. Jobs will be hard to find in small and nonprofit theaters, since these organizations are cutting their budgets or doing smaller shows that require fewer costumes. There may be more opportunities in cable television and independent motion picture industries, which are growing rapidly and will continue to expand in the next decade. New York City and Hollywood are the main centers for costume designers.

Dancers and Choreographers

What Dancers and Choreographers Do

Dancers use body movements to tell a story, express an idea or feeling, or entertain their audiences. Most dancers study some ballet or classical dance. *Classical dance* training gives dancers a good foundation for most other types of dance. Many of the standard dance terms used in all types of dance are the same terms used in 17th-century ballet.

Modern dance developed early in the 20th century as a departure from classical ballet. Early modern dancers danced barefoot and began to explore movement and physical expression in new ways. *Jazz dance* is a form of modern dance often seen in Broadway productions. *Tap dance* combines sound and movement as

Profile: Twyla Tharp

Dancer and choreographer Twyla Tharp became known for her imaginative works that combine modern and traditional dance movements. *Eight Jelly Rolls*, *Push Comes to Shove*, and *Bach Partita* are some of her works.

Tharp was born in Portland, Indiana, and studied music and dance as a child. While attending Barnard College in New York City, she studied dance with Merce Cunningham, Martha Graham, and others. Tharp first danced professionally with the Paul Taylor dance company from 1963 to 1965. She formed her own company in 1965 and also choreographed dances for the Joffrey Ballet, American Ballet Theatre, and other dance companies. She choreographed the motion pictures *Hair* and *Amadeus*. She directed and choreographed the Broadway musicals *Singin' in the Rain* and *Movin' Out*.

Dancers must practice for many hours to achieve the effect of effortless perfection during performance. (Carnegie-Mellon University)

dancers tap out rhythms with metal cleats attached to the toes and heels of their shoes. Other dance forms include ballroom dance, folk or ethnic dance, and acrobatic dance.

Dancers who create new ballets or dance routines are called *choreographers*. Choreographers have a thorough understanding of dance and music, as well as costume, lighting, and dramatics. Besides inventing new dance routines, choreographers teach their dances to performers and sometimes they direct and stage the presentation of their dances.

Choreographers know how to use movement and music to tell a story, create a mood, express an idea, or celebrate movement itself. Since dance is so closely related to music, choreographers must know about various musical styles and rhythms. They often hear a piece of music first and then choreograph a dance to it. Sometimes choreographers plan the dance and then choose the dancers and teach them movements. But most often they work

How Do You Copyright Choreography?

A painting, a novel, a symphony, and other artistic works can be copyrighted to protect them from being stolen and used without the permission of the artists who created them. But how do you copyright choreography? It is difficult to record movements, including gestures and facial expressions, but in order to copyright a dance, there must be some kind of record. These are the methods that can be used to record choreography:

○ video
○ written description
○ drawing stick figures
○ dance notation

Dance notation is the most accurate way to record choreography. The two most common methods are Labanotation, named for its inventor, Rudolphe Laban, and Benesh notation, created by Rudolphe and Joan Benesh.

with their dancers and change the choreography to take best advantage of the dancers' abilities. Choreographers must also be flexible enough to change their dances to fit different performance spaces.

Education and Training

Choreographers almost always start their careers out as dancers. Dancers usually begin training around the age of 10, or even as early as age seven or eight. They may study with private teachers or in ballet schools. Dancers who show promise in their early teens may receive professional training in a regional ballet school or a major ballet company. By the age of 17 or 18, dancers begin to audition for positions in professional dance companies.

Many colleges and universities offer degrees in dance with choreography classes. Although a college degree is not required for dancers and choreographers, it can be helpful. Those who teach dance in a college or university often are required to have a degree.

EXPLORING

○ Take as many dance classes as you can. Try different types of dance with skilled instructors.
○ Once you have learned a dance technique, begin to give recitals and performances.
○ Audition for school or community stage productions that have dance numbers.
○ Try to choreograph a dance routine for a school performance or community event.
○ Watch as many famous dance-oriented movies (*Singin' in the Rain, 42nd Street, Footloose,* or *Chicago*) as you can. Note what you like and dislike about the styles of dance and choreography.

Earnings

The U.S. Department of Labor reports that the median salary for dancers was $21,100 in 2002. The lowest paid 10 percent earned $12,880 or less, while the highest paid 10 percent earned $53,350 or more. That same year, choreographers earned a median salary of $29,470. The lowest earning 10 percent earned $14,000 or less, while the highest earning 10 percent earned $57,590 or more.

Because of the lack of steady, well-paying work, many dancers and choreographers must supplement their income with earnings from other jobs. Possibilities include teaching dance, working several part-time dance jobs, or going outside the field for other work.

Outlook

Job opportunities for dancers and choreographers will have average growth through the next decade. Very few dancers and choreographers work year round, and they often take other jobs to make extra money. More than half the dance companies in the United States are in New York City, which means the majority of dancers and choreographers live there. There are opportunities in other large cities where there are dance companies and theater companies. There is some work available in film and television, too.

FOR MORE INFO

For information on all aspects of dance, including job listings, send a self-addressed, stamped envelope to:
American Dance Guild
31 West 21st Street, 3rd Floor
New York, NY 10010
Tel: 212-627-3790

A directory of dance companies and other information on professional dance is available from Dance/USA.
Dance/USA
1156 15th Street, NW, Suite 820
Washington, DC 20005-1726
Tel: 202-833-1717
Email: danceusa@danceusa.org
http://www.danceusa.org

NDA compiles a dance directory with information on universities, colleges, dance stu-
dios, and high schools that offer dance education and programs.
National Dance Association (NDA)
American Alliance for Health, Physical Education, Recreation & Dance
1900 Association Drive
Reston, VA 20191-1598
Tel: 800-213-7193 ext. 464
http://www.aahperd.org/nda

Visit Dance Magazine's *website to read abstracts of articles that appear in the print version. For general questions, contact*
Dance Magazine
111 Myrtle Street, Suite 203
Oakland, CA 94607
Tel: 510-839-6060
http://www.dancemagazine.com

Film Directors

What Film Directors Do

Film directors, also called *filmmakers,* coordinate the making of a film. They work with actors, costume designers, camera operators, lighting designers, and producers. Directors are involved in everything from hiring actors to helping edit the final film.

While *producers* are in charge of the business and financial side of a film project, directors are in charge of the creative and technical side. Usually a producer hires the director, but they work closely together. They plan a budget and production schedule, including time for research, filming, and editing.

Directors work with scriptwriters, actors, studio technicians, and set designers. They give directions to many different people. They choose costumes, scenery, and music. During rehearsals, they plan the action carefully, telling actors how to move and interpret the script. They coach the actors to help them give their best performances. At the same time, directors give directions for sets and lighting, and decide on the order and angles of camera shots. Once filming is finished, they supervise film editing and add sound and special effects.

Learn at Camp

Many camps and workshops offer programs for students interested in film work. For example, the University of Wisconsin offers its Summer Art Studio for students in grades 7–12. In addition to film courses, there are classes in drawing, painting, photography, and television and video.

For information, visit http://www.uwgb.edu/outreach/camps or write to the University of Wisconsin-Green Bay, Office of Outreach, 2420 Nicolet Drive, Green Bay, WI 54311-7001.

Most directors specialize in one type of film, such as documentaries, feature films, industrial films, and travelogues.

Education and Training

You can start now to prepare for a career in film directing. Take English literature classes to learn storytelling techniques. Theater classes will teach you about acting. Photography courses can teach you about visual composition.

EXPLORING

○ Watch movies every chance you get, both at the theater and at home. Notice what makes them interesting, from camera angles to soundtrack choices.

○ Two major trade publications to read are *Variety* (http://www.variety.com) and *Hollywood Reporter* (http://www.hollywoodreporter.com).

Even though there are no specific requirements for becoming a film director, the most successful directors have a wide variety of talents and experience, as well as good business and management skills. You must be able to develop ideas, and be good at communicating with others.

There are many colleges and universities that offer film majors with concentration in directing. These programs require you to direct your own films. They also offer internship and other practical learning experiences. George Lucas's first film, *THX 1138*, was adapted from a short film he made as a student at the University of Southern California film school. The Directors Guild of America offers an Assistant Directors Training Program for those who have a bachelor's degree or two years of experience in movie production. (See the end of this chapter for more information.)

Many directors begin at small television stations or community theaters, or as production assistants for films. Many directors have worked for a number of years as actors, or in some other capacity within the industry, to gain experience.

And the Oscar Goes To . . .

The Academy of Motion Picture Arts and Sciences awarded Oscars to these directors in recent years:

2003: Peter Jackson, *The Lord of the Rings: The Return of the King*

2002: Roman Polanski, *The Pianist*

2001: Ron Howard, *A Beautiful Mind*

2000: Steven Soderbergh, *Traffic*

1999: Sam Mendes, *American Beauty*

1998: Steven Spielberg, *Saving Private Ryan*

1997: James Cameron, *Titanic*

1996: Anthony Minghella, *The English Patient*

1995: Mel Gibson, *Braveheart*

Earnings

The median annual salary of film producers and directors is $46,240. Among all directors, the lowest paid 10 percent earned less than $23,300, and the highest paid 10 percent earned more than $119,760.

FOR MORE INFO

For a list of film schools and articles about the film industry, visit the AFI website.

American Film Institute (AFI)
2021 North Western Avenue
Los Angeles, CA 90027
Tel: 323-856-7600
http://www.afionline.org

For information about the Assistant Directors Training Program, contact

Directors Guild of America/Assistant Directors Training Program
14724 Ventura Boulevard, Suite 775
Sherman Oaks, CA 91403
Tel: 818-386-2545
http://www.trainingplan.org

Directors' salaries vary greatly. Most Hollywood film directors are members of the Directors Guild of America; this union usually negotiates salaries, hours of work, and other employment conditions. Keep in mind that because directors are freelancers, they may have no income for many weeks out of the year.

Outlook

Because of an increase in the cable television and video-rental industries, the employment outlook for film directors is good. Employment should grow faster than average through the coming years. However, many people are interested in becoming directors and there will be stiff competition for jobs.

Film Editors

What Film Editors Do

Film editors use special equipment to alter an unedited movie or videotape and arrange the material to create the most effective film possible. They work with producers and directors from the earliest phases of filming and production. In meetings with producers, editors learn about the objectives of the film or video. The producer may explain the larger scope of the project so that the editor knows the best way to approach the work when it is time to edit the film. With the director, editors discuss the objective and story line of the film or video. They may discuss scenes and camera angles before filming even begins so that the editor understands the director's vision of the final piece.

Once filming is complete, film editors rate and choose the segments that will be used. Sometimes there are five or 10 takes of one scene, and editors select segments in terms of film or video quality, dramatic value, or other criteria. Editors refer to the script and the director's notes when making their choices. They time the film or video segments to specified lengths and reassemble the segments in a sequence so that they have the greatest effect and make the most sense. Editors and directors review the reassembled material on a video

And the Oscar Goes To . . .

The following film editors have recently won Oscars for their work in recent years:

2003: James Selkirk, *The Lord of the Rings: The Return of the King*

2002: Martin Walsh, *Chicago*

2001: Pietro Scalia, *Black Hawk Down*

2000: Stephen Mirrone, *Traffic*

1999: Zach Staenberg, *The Matrix*

1998: Michael Kahn, *Saving Private Ryan*

monitor, and editors make further adjustments and corrections until the final product is satisfactory to the director and producer. Editing a feature film or documentary can take six to nine months.

Film editors today use nonlinear processes more often. In this type of process, the film is transferred to a digital format. A computer database tracks individual frames and puts all the scenes together in a folder of information. This information is stored on a computer hard drive and can be brought up instantly on a screen, allowing the editor to access scenes and frames with the click of a mouse.

Sound editors work on film soundtracks. They often keep libraries of sounds that they frequently use for various projects, including natural sounds such as thunder or raindrops, animal noises, motor sounds, or musical interludes. Some sound editors specialize in music, and others work with sound effects. They may use unusual objects, machines, or computer-generated noisemakers to create a desired sound for a film.

EXPLORING

- ○ Join a film or video club at your school or community center.
- ○ Research different kinds of film projects, including documentaries, short films, and feature films.
- ○ Experiment with one of the many digital film editing systems available for home computers. You can feed your own digital video into your computer, edit the material, and then add your own special effects and titles.

Education and Training

Training to work as a film editor takes many years. A liberal arts education is the best preparation for this career. Some studios require their editors to have a bachelor's degree. English, journalism, theater, or film are good majors to pursue. Some community and two-year colleges offer film study programs with courses in film and video editing. Universities with departments of broadcast journalism offer courses in

Try It!

Visit the DigiPuppet website (http://www.digipuppet.com) to view and edit two scenes of actual film footage. (Note: You will need one of the following home computer editing programs: iMovie 4, Final Cut Pro, Final Cut Express 2, Adobe Premiere 4.2, orAvid Free DV.)

film and video editing and also may have contacts at local television stations. The American Film Institute offers listings of colleges with film courses and graduate film schools.

Apprenticeships provide good exposure to the day-to-day work of film and television editing. By working closely with an editor, an apprentice can learn film operations and specific film-editing techniques.

FOR MORE INFO

The ACE features some career and education information for film editors on its website, along with information about internship opportunities and sample articles from Cine-maEditor magazine.

American Cinema Editors (ACE)
100 Universal City Plaza
Building 2282, Room 234
Universal City, CA 91608
Tel: 818-777-2900
http://www.ace-filmeditors.org

For information about AFI's Conservatory's master of fine arts in editing and to read

interviews with professionals, visit the AFI website.

American Film Institute (AFI)
2021 North Western Avenue
Los Angeles, CA 90027
Tel: 323-856-7600
http://www.afi.com

For an overview of film editing and useful exercises, visit the following website:

Film Editing: Manipulating Time and Space
http://www.oscars.org/teachersguide/
filmediting/download.html

Earnings

Film editors are not as highly paid as others working in their industry. They have less clout than directors or producers, but they have more authority in the production of a project than many other film industry workers. The median annual income for film editors is $38,270. A small percentage of film editors earn less than $20,030 a year, while some earn more than $78,070. The most experienced and sought-after film editors can command very high salaries.

Outlook

Employment of film editors is expected to grow faster than the average in the next decade. The growth of cable television and an increase in the number of independent film studios will increase the demand for editors.

The digital revolution has affected the editing process greatly. Editors work much more closely with special effects experts in putting together projects. Digital technology creates more direct routes into the industry for prospective editors, but the majority of editors will have to follow traditional routes, obtaining years of experience.

Film Producers

What Film Producers Do

The primary responsibility of *film producers* is to organize and secure money to make films. The job of a producer begins with the selection of a movie idea from a script or other material. Some films are made from original screenplays, and others are adapted from books. If a book is selected, the producer first purchases the rights from the author or publishing company and hires a writer to adapt the book into a screenplay.

After selecting a project, the producer finds a director, technical crew, and lead actors to participate in the film. Along with the script and screenwriter, these essential people are referred to as the package. It is the package that the producer tries to sell to an investor to raise the necessary funds to finance the film.

There are three common sources for financing a film: major studios, production companies, and individual investors. Major studios are the largest source of money and finance most of the big-budget films. Producers of documentary films approach individual donors; foundations; art agencies of federal, state, and local governments; and even family members and religious organizations.

Raising money from individual investors can occupy much of the producer's time. Fund-raising is done on the telephone as well as in conferences, at business lunches, and even at cocktail parties.

On the Web

Visit this Scholastic site to read about the making and the people behind the *Spy Kids* movies. Meet the Magic Makers of *Spy Kids 3D: Game Over*
http://teacher.scholastic.com/scholasticnews/indepth/3d

After raising the money, the producer takes the basic plan of the package and tries to work it into a developed project. The script may be rewritten several times, a full cast of actors is hired, salaries are negotiated, and the filming location is chosen.

During the production phase, the producer tries to keep the project on schedule and expenses within the established budget. Other production tasks include the review of dailies, which are prints of the day's filming. As the head of the project, the producer is responsible for resolving all problems, including personal conflicts such as those between the director and an actor, or the director and the studio. When the film is complete, the producer monitors its distribution and may participate in the publicity and advertising of the film.

Education and Training

English composition and speech courses will help you develop writing and communication skills. Business and economics courses can prepare you for the financial responsibilities of a producer's job.

Exploring

- Join a film or video club.
- Get involved in your school's theater productions, especially in a fund-raising capacity
- Volunteer to work on committees that organize, produce, and publicize special events at your school or religious center.

Many film producers have taken formal courses at a college or a university or have been through special film programs. There are more than 1,000 colleges, universities, and trade schools that offer classes in film studies. However, experience is the best qualification for this job. Most producers work their way into the position from other film-related jobs, such as production, acting, editing, and directing. It is important to have contacts in the industry and with potential investors.

Film History

Motion picture cameras were invented in the late 1800s. The two earliest known films were made in 1888 by French-born Louis Le Prince. They showed his father-in-law's garden and traffic crossing an English bridge.

More advanced cameras and motion picture techniques quickly followed. In 1903 American director Edwin Porter and inventor Thomas Edison made *The Great Train Robbery*, one of the first movies in which scenes were filmed out of sequence; when the filming was completed, the scenes were edited and spliced together. By 1906, feature-length films were being made and many talented and money-smart people were making their livings as producers. The first woman to become a producer was Alice Guy, who started the Solax Company in New York in 1910.

Earnings

Film producers are generally paid a percentage of the project's profits or a fee negotiated between the producer and a studio. Producers in the motion picture and video industries earn an average of $75,440. Salaries for all producers range from less than $23,300 to more than $119,760. Producers of highly successful films can earn $200,000 or more, while those who make low-budget documentary films might earn considerably less than the average. Entry-level *production assistants* can earn from less than minimum wage to $15,000 per year.

Outlook

Employment for film producers is expected to grow faster than the average in the coming years. Opportunities may increase with the expansion of cable and satellite television, video and

DVD rentals, and an increased overseas demand for American-made films, but competition for jobs will be strong. Live theater and entertainment will also provide job openings.

FOR MORE INFO

For film news and information on educational programs, visit the AFI website or contact

American Film Institute (AFI)
2021 North Western Avenue
Los Angeles, CA 90027
Tel: 323-856-7600
http://www.afi.com

Visit the FAQ section of the PGA website to read about producer careers.

Producers Guild of America (PGA)
8530 Wilshire Boulevard, Suite 450
Beverly Hills, CA 90211
Tel: 310-358-9020
http://www.producersguild.org

Lighting Technicians

What Lighting Technicians Do

Lighting technicians set up and control the lighting equipment for movie and television productions. These technicians are sometimes known as *assistant chief set electricians* or *lights operators*. The head lighting technician is known as a *gaffer.*

When a movie shoot is being planned, lighting technicians talk with the director to find out what types of lighting and special lighting effects will be used. Lighting technicians then arrange the equipment they will need to produce the required lighting effects. For example, if the script calls for sunshine to be streaming through a window, technicians set up lights to produce this effect. Other effects they may be asked to produce include lighting the flash from an explosion or the soft glow of a room lit with old-fashioned oil lamps.

The amount of work done by lighting technicians depends on the movie's budget. If the production is small, the technicians will set up the lights themselves. For blockbuster movie shoots, assistants set up the lights following the lighting technician's instructions.

During the filming, lighting technicians work in a control room and follow a special script. The script tells them which lighting effects are needed at what times during the shoot. During filming, the lighting technicians watch the shoot on television monitors in the control room. This enables them to see their work and to make adjustments.

On the Web

Visit this site to explore different theater jobs and play an interactive game about lighting a scene.

Kids Work!

http://www.knowitall.org/kidswork/theater/jobplay/ltdesigner

Setting up lights can be hard work, especially when lighting a large movie set. Technicians should be able to handle heavy lights on stands and work with suspended lights while on a ladder. They should be able to work with electricians' hand tools (screwdrivers, pliers, and so forth) and be comfortable working with electricity. Lighting technicians should also be dependable and capable of working as part of a team.

Education and Training

In high school, you should learn as much as possible about electronics, film history, and working with cameras. Courses in physics and math are also important. Good communication skills are essential for working with the various people on the movie set.

After high school, seek out community colleges and technical schools that offer programs in electronics and broadcast technology. If you would like to rise to a technical management position, you should consider earning a college degree in electrical or electronics engineering.

Earnings

Salaries for lighting technicians vary according to the technician's experience. Annual income is also determined by the number of projects a technician handles during a year. The most experienced technicians can work year-round on a variety of projects, while those starting out may go weeks without work. According to the International Alliance of Theater Stage Engineers, the union that represents lighting technicians, the minimum

EXPLORING

○ Work the lighting for a school stage production.
○ Join your school's newspaper or yearbook staff and practice working with cameras. Experiment with different lighting options.
○ Ask if you can record a school play, concert, or sporting event. Before the event, figure out what lighting will be used and how best to film it.

Tools of the Trade

Need a baby-baby? A midget? A nooklite? An inbetweenie? Visit http://www.mole.com, the website for the Mole-Richardson Company, to read about lighting equipment used in Hollywood. Here you can browse an online catalog that has pictures of different kinds of lighting products and get a sense of some of the lingo of the profession.

hourly pay for unionized gaffers was $22.50 in 2000. Other lighting technicians earned at least $16.50 to $20.50 an hour. Experienced technicians can negotiate for much higher wages.

Outlook

As long as the movie and television industries continue to grow, there will be job opportunities for lighting technicians. With the expansion of the cable market, lighting technicians may find work in more than one industry. However, persistence and hard work are required to secure a good job in film. The increasing use of visual effects and computer-generated

FOR MORE INFO

To read interviews with filmmakers, visit the AFI website.

American Film Institute (AFI)
2021 North Western Avenue
Los Angeles, CA 90027
Tel: 323-856-7600
http://www.afi.com

Visit this site for interviews with award-winning cinematographers, a "tricks of the trade" page, information about film schools, multimedia presentations, and the American Cinematographer *online magazine.*

American Society of Cinematographers
PO Box 2230
Hollywood, CA 90078
Tel: 800-448-0145
http://www.theasc.com

imagery will likely have an impact on the work of lighting technicians. Through computer programs, filmmakers and editors can adjust lighting themselves. However, live-action shots are still integral to the filmmaking process and will remain so for some time. Getting the initial shots of a film requires sophisticated lighting equipment and trained technicians. Lighting technicians often have to know about the assembly and operation of more pieces of equipment than anyone else working on a production. In the future, equipment will become more compact and mobile, making the technician's job easier.

Media Planners and Buyers

What Media Planners and Buyers Do

Media specialists place advertisements that will reach targeted customers and get the best response for the least amount of money. Within the media department, *media planners* gather information about the sizes and types of audiences that can be reached through each of the various media and about the cost of advertising in each medium. *Media buyers* purchase space in printed publications, on billboards and the Internet, and on radio or television stations. Advertising media workers are supervised by a *media director,* who is responsible for the overall media plan. In addition to advertising agencies, media planners and buyers work for large companies, such as film studios, that purchase space or broadcast time. These media specialists must be familiar with the markets that each medium reaches, as well as the advantages and disadvantages of advertising in each.

Media planners determine target markets based on their clients' advertising needs. For example, if a movie studio wanted to advertise its new *Harry Potter* movie, media planners would gather information about the public's viewing, reading, and buying

Personal and Professional Skills

The following skills are useful for media planners and buyers:

- ○ strong understanding of film industry and consumer buying trends
- ○ problem-solving abilities
- ○ creativity
- ○ excellent oral, written, and analytical skills
- ○ ability to handle multiple assignments

habits by administering questionnaires and conducting other forms of market research. Through this research, planners would identify target markets (in this case, children, readers of the *Harry Potter* books, etc.) by sorting data according to people's ages, incomes, marital status, interests, and leisure activities.

By knowing which groups of people watch certain shows, listen to specific radio stations, or read particular magazines or newspapers, media planners can help the movie studio select air time or print space to reach the consumers most likely to watch the movie. For example, Saturday morning television shows attract children, while prime-time programs often draw family audiences. These would be excellent places to advertise the new *Harry Potter* movie since these groups make up a large segment of potential viewers.

Media buyers purchase time on radio or television or the space in a newspaper or magazine in which an advertisement will run. Media buyers make sure that ads appear when and where they should, negotiate costs, and calculate rates, usage, and budgets. They also maintain contact with clients.

Workers who actually sell the print space or air time to advertisers are called *print sales workers* or *broadcast time salespeople*. Like media planners, these professionals know much about their target markets and can often provide useful information about editorial content or broadcast programs.

Interactive media specialists are responsible for managing all critical aspects of their clients' online advertising campaigns. While interactive media planners may have responsibilities similar to those of print or broadcast planners, they also act as new

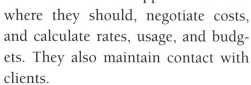

EXPLORING

○ Work as a production assistant, programmer, writer, or editor in your school's media department.

○ Work as an advertising salesperson for your school's yearbook or theater department.

○ Volunteer or work part time for the classified advertising department of your local newspaper.

○ Choose a popular movie and determine its target audience and the best advertising methods to reach this group of people.

Words to Learn

advertisement   paid announcement of a product or service to the public

advertising agency   group of researchers, writers, artists, buyers of space and time, other account executives, and other specialists who design and execute advertising programs for clients

electronic banners   Internet equivalent of billboard advertising, which accounts for 80 percent of online ads

market research   study of consumer groups to determine personal interests and characteristics

media   avenues through which advertisers can place ads, including the Internet, television, radio, magazines, newspapers, and outdoor signs

target audience   group of consumers that is considered the most likely to purchase a product; also known as target market

time slot   specific time that a commercial will air on television or radio

technology specialists, placing and tracking all online ads and maintaining relationships with clients and webmasters alike.

Education and Training

In high school, take courses in business, marketing, advertising, radio and television, and film and video. General liberal arts classes, such as economics, English, communication, and journalism, are also important, since good communication skills are a must. Mathematics classes provide the skills to work with budget figures and placement costs.

Most media planners and buyers have college degrees, often with majors in marketing or advertising. Even if you have prior work experience or training in media, you should select college classes that provide a good balance of business course work, broadcast and print experience, and liberal arts studies.

Earnings

Because media planners and buyers work for a variety of organizations in many locations, their earnings can vary greatly. Advertising sales agents have median annual earnings of $37,670. Salaries range from less than $19,430 to more than $87,560. Media directors can earn between $46,000 and $120,000, depending on the type of employer and the director's experience level.

Some salespeople draw straight salaries, some receive bonuses that reflect their level of sales, and still others earn their entire salary based on commissions. These commissions are usually calculated as a percentage of sales that the employee brings into the company.

Outlook

The employment outlook for media planners and buyers, like the outlook for the advertising industry itself, depends on the general health of the economy. When the economy thrives, companies produce an increasing number of goods and seek to promote them via newspapers, magazines, television, radio, the Internet, and various other media. Employment in the advertising industry is projected to grow much faster than the average for all occupations.

Competition for all advertising positions, including entry-level jobs, is expected to be intense. Media planners and buyers who have considerable experience will have the best chances of finding employment.

FOR MORE INFO

For information on the advertising industry, contact
American Advertising Federation (AAF)
1101 Vermont Avenue, NW, Suite 500
Washington, DC 20005
Tel: 202-898-0089
http://www.aaf.org

Music Directors and Conductors

What Music Directors and Conductors Do

Orchestras, operas, choirs, and bands are groups of musicians who make music together. *Conductors* are the men and women who direct musicians as they play. Conductors sometimes carry the title of *music director,* which implies a wider area of responsibilities, including administrative and managerial duties.

Music directors and conductors have many responsibilities. Their most important task is deciding how a piece of music should be played and then teaching the musicians in the orchestra to play the piece that way. In other words, they help the orchestra or choir interpret a piece of music.

In addition to interpreting music, music directors and conductors help groups play as a unit. A symphony orchestra, for example, may have 50–80 musicians who play a variety of instruments. Each group of instruments, such as violins or French horns, has a slightly different musical line to play. Without a strong conductor, it would be difficult for all these musicians to produce a pleasing sound. The conductor sets the beat, decides when the music should be played louder or softer, and indicates which

On the Web

The American Federation of Musicians of the United States and Canada hosts a Young Musician Page (http://www.afm.org/public/musicians). Check it out for career and educational advice on how to break into the music business.

EXPLORING

○ Go to as many musical presentations as you can—symphonies, operas, musical theater—and study the conductors and directors. Note their baton techniques and their arm and body movements. Try to determine how the orchestra and audience respond to the gesturing of the conductors.

○ Join your school band.

○ Ask your music teacher if he or she can arrange a class trip to the symphony or set up an interview between you and a professional conductor.

instruments should play at what times.

Conductors work with many different types of musical groups. Some lead symphony orchestras. Others direct orchestras that play during operas, musical plays, or ballet performances. Conductors also lead marching bands, jazz bands, and dance bands.

Music directors and conductors must have the complete respect of the musicians they lead. Their jobs are unique in the modern musical world in that they make no sound themselves yet control the sounds that others make.

Education and Training

To be a director or conductor, you should have formal training in at least one musical instrument. You must know music theory, analysis, composition, notation, and sight reading. You need the skills to control the timing, rhythm, and structure of a musical piece. You must also command the attention and respect of orchestra members.

Most directors and conductors study music throughout their lives. Many of the conductor's skills are learned and developed in practice. But formal training is also important. Some conservatories (special music schools) and universities offer conducting programs. Some schools offer courses in music and music appreciation. Other helpful classes include math, dance, and theater. Many schools have student bands and orchestras. However, serious music students usually

Books to Read

Reference books and biographies can give you insight into conductors and their work. Here are some suggestions:

Boonshaft, Peter Loel. *Teaching Music with Passion: Conducting, Rehearsing, and Inspiring*. Galesville, Md.: Meredith Music, 2002.

Burt, George. *The Art of Film Music*. Boston: Northeastern University Press, 1996.

McElheran, Brock. *Conducting Technique for Beginners and Professionals*. London: Oxford University Press, 1989.

Rudolph, Max. *The Grammar of Conducting*. Belmont, Calif.: Wadsworth Publishing Company, 1995.

Scherchen, Herman. *Handbook of Conducting*. London: Oxford University Press, 1990.

attend conservatories. Students also study with private teachers.

Earnings

The range of earnings for musical directors and conductors is enormous. For instance, many conductors work only part time and make small yearly incomes for their conducting endeavors. Part-time choir directors for churches and temples, for instance, make from $3,500 to $25,000 per year, while full-time directors make from $15,000 to $40,000 per year. Conductors of dance bands make from $300 to $1,200 per week. Opera and choral group conductors make as little as $8,000 per year working part time at the community level, but salaries range to over $100,000 per year for those with permanent positions with established companies in major cities. The same applies to symphony orchestra conductors who, for instance, make

$25,000–$40,000 per year conducting smaller, regional orchestras, but who can make $500,000 or more if they become the resident conductor of an internationally famous orchestra.

Musical directors and conductors who are employed in the motion picture and video industries earn average annual salaries of $68,980.

Outlook

The number of music directing and conducting jobs is expected to grow at an average rate in the next decade. The overall number of orchestras in the United States has grown only slightly in the last two decades. The number of orchestras in academic settings declined slightly, while community, youth, and city orchestras increased slightly in number. The slight growth pattern of orchestra groups will not nearly accommodate the number of people who graduated from music school during that period and are trying to become conductors. The competition for music conductor and director jobs should become even more fierce over the next decade. Only the most talented people moving into the field will be able to find full-time jobs.

FOR MORE INFO

For industry news and audition information, contact
American Guild of Musical Artists
1430 Broadway, 14th Floor
New York, NY 10018
Tel: 212-265-3687
http://www.musicalartists.org

For information on orchestra management careers, contact
American Symphony Orchestra League
33 West 60th Street, 5th Floor
New York, NY 10023
Tel: 212-262-5161
http://www.symphony.org

For information on auditions and competitions in Canada, contact
Orchestras Canada
56 The Esplanade, Suite 203
Toronto, ON M5E 1A7
Canada
Tel: 416-366-8834
http://www.oc.ca

Production Assistants

What Production Assistants Do

Production assistants (PAs) perform a variety of tasks for film, television, and video producers and other staff members. Their work is not glamorous, but it provides valuable experience and contacts in other areas of the industry.

Production assistants' duties range from making sure a Hollywood star has coffee in the morning to stopping street traffic so a director can film a scene. They photocopy scripts for actors, help set up equipment, and perform other menial tasks. The best PAs know where to be at the right time to make themselves useful.

Some production assistants are responsible for keeping production files in order. These files include contracts, budgets, page changes (old pages from a script that has been revised), and other records. The documents must be kept organized and accessible for whenever the producer may need them.

Production assistants may also have to keep the producer's production folder in order and up to date. The production folder contains everything the producer needs to know about the production at a glance. PAs make sure the folder includes the shooting schedule, the most recent

> ### Words to Learn
>
> **breakdown script** list of cast members and items, such as production equipment and props, required for that day's shoot
>
> **call sheet** list of the actors needed for each scene.
>
> **craft service** working with the caterer, craft service provides snacks for cast and crew during a production
>
> **hot set** set on which filming is currently taking place
>
> **swing gang** construction team that builds and breaks down a set

version of the budget, cast and crew lists with phone numbers, a phone sheet detailing all production-related phone calls the producer needs to make, and the up-to-date shooting script. As new versions of these forms are created, PAs update the producer's folder and file the older versions for reference.

PAs schedule an hour or so in a producer's schedule to watch the dailies (the film shot each day) and make related calls to discuss them with other staff members. PAs make travel and hotel reservations and arrange for rehearsal space. They run errands and communicate messages for producers, directors, actors, musicians, and other members of the technical crew.

PAs often get stuck with undesirable tasks such as sweeping floors, guarding movie sets, or finding a particular brand of green tea for a demanding actor. However, a successful film shoot could not happen without production assistants on the set.

Education and Training

To prepare for a career in film, take courses in photography, film, broadcast journalism, and media to learn about the film industry. However, there are no formal education requirements for production assistants. Most PAs consider the position a stepping stone into other careers in the industry. You learn much of what you'll need to know on the set of a film, following the instructions of crew members and other assistants. Many film students work part time or on a contract basis as while they are still in school. A listing of film schools

EXPLORING

○ Join a film club at your school or community center.
○ Get involved in school and community theater productions, working either on stage or behind the curtain.
○ Look for volunteer opportunities at a local theater or on a low-budget film project.
○ Read about the film industry in such publications as *Daily Variety* (http://www.variety.com) and *Hollywood Reporter* (http://www.hollywoodreporter.com).

All in a Day's Work

If you still want a production assistant job after reading this list, you may just have what it takes to succeed. Here are some possible tasks on any given day:

○ purchasing, washing, chopping, and arranging 20 pounds of fruits and veggies for the cast and crew snack table
○ purchasing $200 worth of extra fancy ketchup and then submerging an actor's costume in it
○ watching videotapes for hours to make sure that there aren't any technical glitches
○ leaving the set every hour to insert more quarters in the meter where the director's car is parked
○ driving around the city all day delivering scripts.
○ cleaning up dog/cat/horse/cheetah/lizard "messes" after an animal show
○ sitting around, doing absolutely nothing

is available from the American Film Institute. There are many good undergraduate programs in film and video with concentrations in such areas as directing, acting, editing, producing, screenwriting, cinematography, broadcast engineering, and television.

Earnings

Because working as a PA is the starting point for most professionals and artists in the film industry, many people volunteer their time until they make connections and move into paid positions. Those assistants who can negotiate payment may make between $200 and $400 a week, but they may only have the opportunity to work on a few projects a year. PAs working full time in an office may start at around $20,000 a year, but with experience they can make around $65,000.

FOR MORE INFO

For information about colleges with film and television programs of study, and to read interviews with filmmakers, visit the AFI website.

American Film Institute (AFI)
2021 North Western Avenue
Los Angeles, CA 90027
Tel: 323-856-7600
http://www.afi.com

To read selected articles from American Cinematographer *magazine, visit the ASC website.*

American Society of Cinematographers (ASC)
PO Box 2230
Hollywood, CA 90078
Tel: 800-448-0145
http://www.theasc.com

Outlook

There will always be a need for assistants in film production. However, competition for jobs can be tough, since this is a good entry-level position for someone who wants to make connections and learn about the film industry. Fortunately, PAs usually do not stay in their jobs more than one or two years, so turnover is fairly high. PAs will find employment anywhere a motion picture, television show, or video is being filmed, but more opportunities exist in Los Angeles and New York City. There may be opportunities at local television stations or smaller production companies that produce educational and corporate videos.

Production Designers

What Production Designers Do

Production designers are responsible for the visual aspects of films, videos, and television commercials. These include sets, props, costumes, makeup, special effects, landscaping, and any other resources that help tell a story or set a mood. Production designers work with directors and producers to interpret scripts and create or select settings in order to visually convey the story. They oversee set decorators and designers, model makers, location managers, propmasters, construction coordinators, and special effects workers. In addition, production designers work with writers, unit production managers, cinematographers, costume designers, and post-production staff, including editors and employees responsible for scoring and titles.

Before filming begins, the production designer prepares a plan that details his or her artistic vision for the motion picture. They read the script to get a better idea of the movie's theme and setting. They meet with directors and producers to discuss the overall look and feel of the movie, learn more about historical details of the film, such as clothing or interior design, and scout potential filming locations. They also create a budget for the production.

To illustrate the look of each scene in a movie, production design-

> **Top Skills for Production Designers**
>
> - creativity
> - imagination
> - attention to detail
> - teamwork
> - strong communication skills
> - knowledge of the arts and history

EXPLORING

○ Develop your "creative eye," that is, your ability to develop ideas visually by watching award-winning motion pictures, videos, and commercials.

○ Volunteer to assist with set design and props for a school play or community theatre productions.

○ Research and film a historical scene or movie using a handheld video recorder. Ask yourself the following questions: What type of costumes (style, color, etc.) did people of this era wear? What did a typical room, street, or town look like? What other settings do I need to create or construct? What props should I use to make the scene believable to the viewer?

ers and their staff create storyboards, sketches, blueprints, technical drawings, and three-dimensional models. They show these to the film's director and producer, cinematographer, head costume designer, and head makeup artist to ensure that they share the same vision for the film. Once the plan and project budget are approved, the production designer sets up a production schedule and begins construction of the sets.

Many production designers work overtime during busy periods in order to meet deadlines. Production designers at film and video operations and at television studios work as many hours as required—usually many more than 40 per week—in order to finish projects on schedule.

Computer technology is changing the way production designers create plans for movies. Many designers now use computer programs to create virtual sets, eliminating the need for storyboards, sketches, models, and other materials.

Education and Training

A variety of high school courses will give you both a taste of college-level offerings and an idea of the skills necessary for work as a production designer. These courses include art, drawing, art history, illustration, photography, mathematics, and desktop publishing. Other useful courses include business, computer science, English, technical drawing, cultural studies, psychology, and social science.

A college degree in film design, interior design, art, architecture, or stage design is usually a requirement for production designers. The American Film Institute Conservatory offers a two-year program in production design (see "For More Info").

Earnings

Salaries for production designers vary based on their level of experience, type of employer, and job location. Production designers in the motion picture and video industries earn median salaries of $107,980. Production designers who are just starting out may earn less than $20,000 annually, while production designers with considerable experience may earn more than $200,000 a year.

Questions, Questions, Questions

When creating a design plan for a motion picture, production designers ask themselves many questions, including:

○ What is the setting for the movie? The past? Present? Future?

○ What type of space or locations will be available for each scene and what is the best design for that space?

○ How will each set look from different camera angles?

○ Does the set allow for easy camera movement?

○ How will each set look with different types of lighting?

○ What props and furnishings (paintings, food, foliage, etc.) will I use to decorate each set?

○ What colors and textures (wall, piece of furniture, costumes, etc.) will I use to define the characters' personalities, moods, and backgrounds?

○ What is my project budget?

FOR MORE INFO

For information on educational opportunities, contact
American Film Institute
Conservatory
2021 North Western Avenue
Los Angeles, CA 90027
http://afi.com/education/conservatory/
productiondesign.aspx

For information on careers in production design and a list of useful books, contact
Art Directors Guild
11969 Ventura Boulevard, Suite 200
Studio City, CA 91604
Tel: 818-762-9995
http://www.artdirectors.org

For information on union representation, contact
International Alliance of Theatrical
Stage Employees, Moving Picture
Technicians, Artists and Allied
Crafts of the United States, Its
Territories and Canada
1430 Broadway, 20th Floor
New York, NY 10018
Tel: 212-730-1770
http://www.iatse-intl.org

For an overview of production design and useful exercises, visit the following website:
Art Direction: The Visual Language
of Film
http://www.oscars.org/teachersguide/
artdirection/download.html

Outlook

Production designers will always be needed to oversee the artistic direction of movies, television shows, and commercials. However, it is important to note that the supply of aspiring production designers is expected to exceed the number of job openings. As a result, those wishing to enter the field will encounter keen competition for jobs. Production designers with proven artistic ability, experience, knowledge of computer design programs, and strong interpersonal skills will have the best employment opportunities.

Screenwriters

What Screenwriters Do

Screenwriters write scripts for motion pictures or television. They may write about themes they choose or story ideas assigned by a producer or director. Screenwriters are often hired to turn popular plays or novels into screenplays. Writers of original screenplays create their own stories that are produced for the motion picture industry or television. Screenwriters may also write television programs, such as comedies, dramas, documentaries, variety shows, and entertainment specials.

Screenwriters must be creative and have excellent research skills. For projects such as historical movies, documentaries, and medical or science programs, research is a critical part of the screenwriter's job.

Screenwriters start with an outline, or a treatment, of the story's plot. When the director or producer approves the story outline, screenwriters then complete the story for production. During the writing process, screenwriters write many drafts of the script. They frequently meet with directors and producers to discuss script changes.

And the Oscar Goes To . . .

The following screenwriters were Oscar winners for best original screenplay:

2003: Sofia Coppola, *Lost in Translation*

2002: Pedro Almodóvar, *Talk to Her*

2001: Julian Fellowes, *Gosford Park*

2000: Cameron Crowe, *Almost Famous*

1999: Alan Ball, *American Beauty*

1998: Marc Norman and Tom Stoppard, *Shakespeare In Love*

1997: Matt Damon and Ben Affleck, *Good Will Hunting*

1996: Ethan Coen and Joel Coen, *Fargo*

1995: Christopher McQuarrie, *The Usual Suspects*

1994: Quentin Tarantino and Roger Avary, *Pulp Fiction*

EXPLORING

○ Read and study as many scripts as you can. Watch a motion picture while following the script at the same time.

○ Read film-industry publications, such as *Daily Variety, Hollywood Reporter,* and *The Hollywood Scriptwriter.*

○ There are a number of books that teach you the format for a screenplay. There are also computer software programs that help with screenplay formatting.

○ Write a play for your classmates or friends to perform.

Some screenwriters work alone and others work with a team of writers. Many specialize in certain types of scripts, such as drama, comedy, documentaries, motion pictures, or television. *Motion-picture screenwriters* usually write alone and exclusively for movies. Screenwriters for television series work very long hours in the studio. Many television shows have limited runs, so much of the work for *television screenwriters* is not continuous.

Education and Training

In high school, you should develop your writing skills in English, theater, speech, and journalism classes. Social studies and foreign language will also help you create intelligent scripts.

A screenwriter must have a good imagination and the ability to tell a story. The best way to prepare for a career as a screenwriter is to write and read every day. A college degree is not required, but a liberal arts education is

On the Web

Visit this site for articles on screenwriting, interviews with famous screenwriters, and information on free online workshops and resources.

Screenwriters Utopia
http://www.screenwritersutopia.com

Women Screenwriters Make History

Women screenwriters were much more prominent in the early days of filmmaking. Half of the films made before 1925 were written by women screenwriters such as Frances Marion (*Stella Dallas, The Scarlet Letter*) and Anita Loos (*The Women*). Marion was the highest paid screenwriter from 1916 to the 1930s, and she served as the first vice president of the Writer's Guild. Though a smaller percentage of feature films written by women are produced today, more women screenwriters have won Academy Awards since 1985 than in all the previous years. Among recent Oscar winners are Ruth Prawer Jhabvala (*A Room With a View* and *Howard's End*), Jane Campion (*The Piano*), Callie Khouri (*Thelma and Louise*), and Emma Thompson (*Sense and Sensibility*).

helpful because it exposes you to a wide range of subjects. While in school, become involved in theater to learn about all of the elements required in a screenplay, such as characters, plots, and themes. Book clubs, creative writing classes, and film study are also good ways to learn the basic elements of screenwriting.

Earnings

Annual wages for screenwriters vary widely. Some screenwriters make hundreds of thousands of dollars from their scripts. Others write and film their own scripts without any payment at all, relying on backers and loans. Screenwriters who work independently do not earn regular salaries. They are paid a fee for each script they write. Those who write for ongoing television shows do earn regular salaries. According to the Writers Guild of America (WGA), the median income for WGA members was $87,104 a year in 2001. Earnings ranged from less than $28,091 to more than $567,726.

FOR MORE INFO

To learn more about the film industry, to read interviews and articles by noted screenwriters, and to find links to many other screenwriting-related sites on the Internet, visit the WGA website.

Writers Guild of America (WGA)
West Chapter
7000 West Third Street
Los Angeles, CA 90048
Tel: 800-548-4532
http://www.wga.org

Writers Guild of America (WGA)
East Chapter
555 West 57th Street, Suite 1230
New York, NY 10019
Tel: 212-767-7800
http://www.wgaeast.org

For an overview of screenwriting and useful exercises, visit the following website:

Screenwriting: The Language of Film
http://www.oscars.org/teachersguide/screenwriting/download.html

Outlook

The job market for screenwriters, especially in film and television, is highly competitive because so many people are attracted to the field. In this industry, it is helpful to network and make contacts. In motion picture screenwriting, and in the creation of new television shows, persistence is important. The growth of the cable industry has increased demand for original screenplays and adaptations.

If you are thinking about becoming a screenwriter, you should also be open to careers in technical writing, journalism, or copywriting. Academic preparation in a related field may help you find another occupation in case a screenwriting job does not happen right away.

Special-Effects Technicians

What Special-Effects Technicians Do

Special-effects technicians make fantastic things seem real in movies, theater, and television. They can make a spaceship fly to distant planets, dangle a car off the edge of a skyscraper, or bring dinosaurs to life on the screen.

Special-effects technicians read scripts and meet with directors to decide on the kinds of effects they will use. Special effects may include computer animation, makeup effects, pyrotechnics, and mechanical effects.

Computer-animation specialists use computer programs to create computer-generated imagery, or CGI, that would otherwise be impossible or too costly to build. These effects make it possible for a human face to change or "morph" into an animal's face, or for a realistic-looking bear to drink a popular soda.

Makeup effects specialists create masks and costumes. They build prosthetic devices, such as human or animal heads or limbs. They must be

And the Oscar Goes To . . .

These films received Oscars in the category of Visual Effects:

2003: *The Lord of the Rings: The Return of the King*

2002: *The Lord of the Rings: The Two Towers*

2001: *The Lord of the Rings: The Fellowship of the Ring*

2000: *Gladiator*

1999: *The Matrix*

1998: *What Dreams May Come*

1997: *Titanic*

1996: *Independence Day*

1995: *Babe*

1994: *Forrest Gump*

Join the Club

S.C.R.E.A.M.—the Student Club of Realistic Effects, Animatronics, and Makeup—is a network of students of all ages who share interest in special effects and the film industry. Its website (http://www.geocities.com/Hollywood/Lot/9373/SCREAM/scream.html) features articles on making teeth and fangs, assembling your own makeup kit, making sugar glass (breakaway glass), and working with zombies, among other topics. There is also a helpful glossary and chat rooms where you can talk to other aspiring film professionals.

skilled at modeling, sewing, applying makeup, and mixing dyes.

Pyrotechnics effects specialists are experts with firearms and explosives. They create explosions for dramatic scenes. This work can be very dangerous. Most states require them to be licensed in order to handle and set off explosives.

Mechanical effects specialists build sets, props, and backgrounds. They build, install, and operate equipment mechanically or electrically. They usually are skilled in carpentry, electricity, welding, and robotics.

Education and Training

To be a special-effects technician you need to know about science and art. Take classes in art, art history, sculpture, chemistry, physics, shop, and computers.

Some universities have film and television programs that offer courses in special effects. Most tech-

EXPLORING

○ Visit your school or public library and bookstores to read more about special effects technology. Look for magazines, such as *Animation Journal, Cinefex, Daily Variety,* and *Hollywood Reporter.*
○ Work on school drama productions as a stagehand, sound technician, or makeup artist.
○ Explore computer animation software programs that allow you to create special effects.
○ If you have a video camera, experiment with special effects in filming and editing.

nicians in the industry say that the best way to enter this career is through experience working on a film crew.

Earnings

Some special-effects technicians have steady, salaried employment, while others work freelance for an hourly rate and may have periods with no work. The average daily rate for beginning technicians is $100–$200 per day, while more experienced technicians can earn $300 per day or more. CGI effects animators have median yearly earnings of around $100,000. On the low end of the scale, these professionals earn around $55,000, and on the high end, $350,000. Effects assistants have beginning wages of around $45,000 and median wages of $60,000.

Two special-effects technicians create a synthetic model of a male accident victim for a feature film. (Corbis)

Read All about It

Hamilton, Jake. *Special Effects in Film and Television.* New York: DK Publishing, 1998.

Netzley, Patricia. *Encyclopedia of Movie Special Effects.* New York: Checkmark Books, 2001.

Rickitt, Richard. *Special Effects: The History and Technique.* New York: Watson-Guptill Publications, 2000.

Timpone, Anthony. *Men, Makeup & Monsters: Hollywood's Masters of Illusion and FX.* New York: St. Martin's Press, 1996.

Vinther, Janus. *Special Effects Make-Up.* New York: Theatre Arts Books, 2003.

FOR MORE INFO

For more information, contact
American Film Institute
2021 North Western Avenue
Los Angeles, CA 90027
Tel: 323-856-7600
http://www.afi.com

For a list of animation schools, lively discussion forums, and general information on the animation industry, visit the AWN website.
Animation World Network (AWN)
6525 Sunset Boulevard, Garden Suite 10
Los Angeles, CA 90028
Tel: 323-606-4200
http://www.awn.com

For information about festivals and industry news, contact
The Visual Effects Society
2308 Broadway
Santa Monica, CA 90404
Tel: 310-315-6055
http://www.visualeffectssociety.com

Outlook

There is strong competition for jobs in this field, and competition will likely increase as the cost of powerful computers and graphics software decreases. More people will be able to develop their own computer animation skills.

Competition for jobs in film special-effects houses is stiff. For more than 25 years now, films of all kinds have used computer graphics and high-tech effects, inspiring a whole generation of young people with computers and imaginations.

Digital technology will continue to change the industry. Experts predict that within 10 years, film will be completely replaced by digital processes, where scenes are recorded on computer chips so they can be further enhanced by computer effects.

Stunt Performers

What Stunt Performers Do

Stunt performers work on film scenes that are risky and dangerous. They act out car crashes and chases, fist and sword fights, and falls from cars, motorcycles, horses, and buildings. They perform airplane and helicopter gags, ride through river rapids, and face wild animals. Some stunt performers specialize in one type of stunt.

There are two general types of stunt roles: *double* and *nondescript*. The first requires a stunt performer to double, or take the place of, a star actor in a dangerous scene. As a double, the stunt performer must portray the character in the same way as the star actor. In a nondescript role, the stunt performer does not stand in for another actor, but plays an incidental character in a dangerous scene. An example of a nondescript role is a driver in a freeway chase scene. Stunt performers rarely have speaking parts.

Directors, especially of large, action-filled movies, often seek the help of a *stunt coordinator*. The stunt coordinator plans the stunt, oversees the setup and construction of special sets and materials, and either hires or recommends the most qualified stunt performer.

Stunt Specialties

Here are some of the skills stunt performers learn in training programs at The United Stuntmen's Association:

- precision driving
- weaponry
- unarmed combat
- horse work
- fire burns
- stair falls
- climbing and repelling
- martial arts
- special effects
- high falls

Famous Daredevils

Stunt performers have been around much longer than the film industry. Throughout the 19th century, circus performers leaped from buildings, walked tightropes, swallowed swords, and stuffed themselves into tiny boxes.

Harry Houdini is one of the most famous showmen in entertainment history. He became internationally renowned by escaping in less than a minute from a chain-wrapped crate that was lowered into New York's East River. Another daredevil was Samuel Gilbert Scott, who showed "extraordinary and surpassing powers in the art of leaping and diving." After swinging about a ship's riggings or jumping from a 240-foot cliff, he would pass around a hat for contributions. His final stunt took place at Waterloo Bridge. While performing pre-dive acrobatics with a rope around his neck, he slipped and strangled to death.

In the 19th century, women daredevils drew as many spectators as the men. Signora Josephine Girardelli was known as the "Fire-Proof Lady." She earned that title by holding boiling oil in her mouth and hands and performing other feats of stamina. Bess Houdini assisted her husband Harry in many famous tricks, including one which ended with her tied up and sealed in a trunk. May Wirth was a talented equestrian, known as "The Wonder Rider of the World" for her somersaults and other stunts while riding a rushing horse.

Although a stunt may last only a few seconds on film, preparations for the stunt can take several hours or even days. Stunt performers work with props, makeup, wardrobe, and set design departments. They also work closely with the special-effects team.

Stunt performers take great care to ensure their safety. They use air bags, body pads, or cables in stunts involving falls or crashes. If a stunt performer must enter a burning building, he or she wears special fireproof clothing and protective cream on the skin.

Education and Training

No standard training exists for stunt performers. They usually start out by contacting stunt coordinators and asking for work.

If the stunt coordinator thinks the person has the proper credentials, he or she will be hired for basic stunt work like fight scenes. There are a number of stunt schools, such as the United Stuntmen's Association National Stunt Training School.

Stunt performers get a lot of training on the job. Every new type of stunt has its own challenges. By working closely with stunt coordinators, you learn how to eliminate most of the risks involved in stunts. Even so, injuries are very common among stunt performers, and there is even the possibility of death in very dangerous stunts.

EXPLORING

○ Stunt performers must be in top physical shape and train like athletes. To develop your physical strength and coordination, play on community sports teams and participate in school athletics.
○ Acting in school or church plays can teach you about taking direction.
○ Theme parks and circuses use stunt performers. Visit these places and try to meet the performers after shows.

Earnings

Stunt performers receive the same day rate as other actors, plus extra pay for more difficult and dangerous stunts. Stunt performers must belong to the actor's union, the Screen Actors Guild (SAG). The SAG minimum day rate was $678 in 2003. A stunt coordinator earned a daily minimum wage of $1,043 in

FOR MORE INFO

For more information on earnings and union representation, contact
Screen Actors Guild
5757 Wilshire Boulevard
Los Angeles, CA 90036
http://www.sag.com

For information about the USA training program and images of stunt performers in action, visit USA's website.
United Stuntmen's Association (USA)
2723 Saratoga Lane
Everett, WA 98203
http://www.stuntschool.com

A stunt performer exits a flipped van after a movie stunt. Stunt performers must have excellent athletic ability and coordination to successfully complete demanding stunts. (Corbis)

2003, and a weekly minimum of $4,118.

Outlook

There are more than 2,500 stunt performers who belong to SAG, but only a small number work on films full time. It is difficult for new stunt performers to break into the business. The future of the profession may be affected by computer technology. Filmmakers today use special effects and computer-generated imagery for action sequences. Computer-generated stunts are also safer. Safety on film sets has always been a serious concern since many stunts are very dangerous. However, using live stunt performers can give a scene more authenticity, so talented stunt performers will always be in demand.

Talent Agents and Scouts

What Talent Agents and Scouts Do

An agent is a salesperson who sells artistic talent. *Talent agents* represent actors, directors, writers, models, and other people who work in film, television, and theater, promoting their talent and managing legal contracts and other business. Talent agents look for clients who have potential for success and then work aggressively to promote their clients to film and television directors, casting directors, production companies, and other potential employers.

Agents find clients in several ways. They review portfolios, screen tests, and audiotapes to evaluate potential clients' appearance, voice, personality, experience, ability to take direction, and other factors. Agents who work for an agency might be assigned a client by the agency, based on experience or a compatible personality. Some agents also work as *talent scouts* and actively search for new clients, whom they then bring to an agency. Or the clients themselves might approach agents who have good reputations and request their representation.

When an agent agrees to represent a client, they both sign a contract that specifies the extent of representation, the time period, payment, and other legal considerations.

Agents also work closely with the potential employers of their clients. They need to satisfy the needs of both parties. Agents who represent actors have a network of directors,

Industry Publications

Daily Variety (http://www.variety.com)

The Hollywood Reporter (http://www.hollywoodreporter.com)

Premiere (http://www.premiere.com)

Entertainment Weekly (http://www.ew.com)

EXPLORING

○ Watch current movies to get a sense of the established and up-and-coming talents in the film industry.

○ Trace the careers of actors you like, including their early work in independent films, commercials, and stage work.

○ Contact a local talent agent to learn more about the career.

producers, advertising executives, and photographers that they contact frequently to see if any of their clients can meet their needs.

When agents see a possible match between employer and client, they speak to both and quickly organize meetings, interviews, or auditions so that employers can meet potential hires and evaluate their work and capabilities. Agents must be persistent and aggressive on behalf of their clients. They spend time on the phone with employers, convincing them of their clients' talents and persuading them to hire clients.

When an employer agrees to hire a client, the agent helps negotiate a contract that outlines salary, benefits, promotional appearances, and other fees, rights, and obligations. Agents have to look out for the best interests of their clients and at the same time satisfy employers in order to establish continuing, long-lasting relationships.

The largest talent agencies are located in Los Angeles and New York City, where the film industry is centered. Independent agents have offices throughout the country.

Education and Training

You should take courses in business, mathematics, and accounting to prepare for the management aspects of an agent's job. Take English and speech courses to develop good communication skills because you will need to be a good negotiator. You also need a good eye for talent, so be sure to develop some expertise in film and related areas.

Although some agents receive their training on the job, a bachelor's degree is strongly recommended for work in this field. Advanced degrees in law and business are becoming increasingly popular since talent agents must write contracts according to legal regulations.

Earnings

Earnings for agents vary greatly, depending on the success of the agent and his or her clients. An agency receives 10–15 percent of a client's fee for a project. An agent is then paid a commission by the agency as well as a base salary. Assistants generally make entry-level salaries of between $18,000 and $20,000 a year. In the first few years, an agent will make between $25,000 and $50,000 a year. However, those working for the top agencies can make much more. Working for an agency, an experienced agent will receive health and retirement benefits, bonuses, and paid travel and accommodations.

Outlook

Although the film industry has enjoyed record box office receipts in recent years, competition for positions as talent agents and scouts is very intense. It may take years and years to become successful in the field, and some aspiring agents

Personal Requirements

Successful talent agents and scouts must have the following traits:

○ good judges of talent
○ strong negotiators
○ hard working and aggressive
○ detail-oriented and business-minded
○ self-motivated
○ ambitious
○ excellent communicators

never make it in the business. On the plus side, overseas markets for U.S. films are expanding, so films that don't do so well in the United States can still turn a tidy profit. Also, more original cable television programming will lead to more actors and performers seeking representation. These expanding markets should create steady opportunities for the most experienced talent agents and scouts.

FOR MORE INFO

For general information on management careers in the performing arts, contact
North American Performing Arts Managers and Agents
459 Columbus Avenue, Suite 133
New York, NY 10024
http://www.napama.org

Visit the SAG website for information about acting in films and for a list of talent agencies.
Screen Actors Guild (SAG)
5757 Wilshire Boulevard
Los Angeles, CA 90036
http://www.sag.com

Glossary

accredited   approved as meeting established standards for providing good training and education; this approval is usually given by an independent organization of professionals to a school or a program in a school

apprentice   person who is learning a trade by working under the supervision of a skilled worker; apprentices often receive classroom instruction in addition to their supervised practical experience

associate's degree   academic rank or title granted by a community or junior college or similar institution to graduates of a two-year program of education beyond high school

bachelor's degree   academic rank or title given to a person who has completed a four-year program of study at a college or university; also called an undergraduate degree or baccalaureate

career   occupation for which a worker receives training and has an opportunity for advancement

certified   approved as meeting established requirements for skill, knowledge, and experience in a particular field; people are certified by the organization of professionals in their field

college   higher education institution that is above the high school level

community college   public two-year college, attended by students who do not usually live at the college; graduates of a community college receive an associate's degree and may transfer to a four-year college or university to complete a bachelor's degree

diploma   certificate or document given by a school to show that a person has completed a course or has graduated from the school

distance education   type of educational program that allows students to take classes and complete their education by mail or the Internet

doctorate   academic rank or title (the highest) granted by a graduate school to a person who has completed a two- to three-year program after having received a master's degree

financial aid   scholarships, loans, and grants provided by government agencies, academic institutions, and professional associations and organizations for academic study

fringe benefit   payment or benefit to an employee in addition to regular wages or salary; examples of fringe benefits include a pension, a paid vacation, and health or life insurance

graduate school   school that people may attend after they have received their bachelor's degree; people who complete an educational program at a graduate school earn a master's degree or a doctorate

grant   financial aid for academic study that does not require repayment; usually awarded based on need

intern   advanced student (usually one with at least some college training) in a professional field who is employed in a job that is intended to provide supervised practical experience for the student

junior college   two-year college that offers courses like those in the first half of a four-year college program; graduates of a junior college usually receive an associate's degree and may transfer to a four-year college or university to complete a bachelor's degree

liberal arts   subjects covered by college courses that develop broad general knowledge rather than specific occupational skills; the liberal arts are often considered to include philosophy, literature and the arts, history, language, and some courses in the social sciences and natural sciences

licensed   having formal permission from the proper authority to carry out an activity that would be illegal without that permission; for example, a person may be licensed to practice medicine or to drive a car

loan   advance of funds for academic study that must be paid back—usually with interest

major (in college)   academic field in which a student specializes and receives a degree

master's degree   academic rank or title granted by a graduate school to a person who has completed a one- or two-year program after having received a bachelor's degree

online education   academic study that is performed by using a computer and the Internet

pension   amount of money paid regularly by an employer to a former employee after he or she retires from working

private   1. not owned or controlled by the government (such as private industry or a private employment agency); **2.** intended only for a particular person or group; not open to all (such as a private road or a private club)

public   1. provided or operated by the government (such as a public library); **2.** open and available to everyone (such as a public meeting)

regulatory   having to do with the rules and laws for carrying out an activity; a regulatory agency, for example, is a government organization that sets up required procedures for how certain things should be done

scholarship   gift of money to a student to help the student pay for further education; see **financial aid**

social studies   courses of study (such as civics, geography, and history) that deal with how human societies work

starting salary   salary paid to a newly hired employee; usually a smaller amount than is paid to a more experienced worker

technical college   private or public college offering two- or four-year programs in technical subjects; technical colleges offer courses in both general and technical subjects and award associate's degrees and bachelor's degrees

technician   worker with specialized practical training in a mechanical or scientific subject who works under the supervision of scientists, engineers, or other professionals; technicians typically receive two years of college-level education after high school

undergraduate   student at a college or university who has not yet received a degree

undergraduate degree   see **bachelor's degree**

union   organization whose members are workers in a particular industry or company; the union works to gain better wages, benefits, and working conditions for its members; also called a labor union or trade union

vocational school   public or private school that offers training in one or more skills or trades

wage   money that is paid in return for work done, especially money paid on the basis of the number of hours or days worked

Index of Job Titles

Browse and Learn More

Books

Clements, Jonathan. *A Kid's Guide to the Movies* (Shortcuts). Somerset, U.K.: Chicken House Publishing Ltd., 2002.

Corey, Melinda, ed. *American Film Institute Desk Reference: The Complete Guide to Everything You Need to Know about the Movies.* New York: DK Publishing, 2002.

Karney, Robyn, Joel Finler, and Ronald Bergan, eds. *Cinema: Year by Year, 1894–2003.* New York: DK Publishing, 2003.

O'Brien, Lisa. *Lights, Camera, Action: Making Movies and TV from the Inside Out.* Owl Communications, 1998.

Osborne, Robert A. *75 Years of the Oscar: The Official History of the Academy Awards.* New York: Abbeville Press, Inc., 2003.

Singleton, Ralph, ed. *Filmmaker's Dictionary.* 2d ed. Los Angeles: Lone Eagle Publishing Company, 2000.

Stoller, Bryan Michael. *Filmmaking For Dummies.* Hoboken, N.J.: Wiley, 2003.

Taub, Eric. *Gaffers, Grips and Best Boys: From Producer-Director to Gaffer* and *Computer Special Effects Creator: A Behind-the-Scenes Look at Who Does What in the Making of a Motion Picture.* New York: St. Martin's Press, 1995.

Websites

Academy of Motion Picture Arts and Sciences
http://www.oscars.org

Acting Workshop On-Line
http://www.redbirdstudio.com/AWOL/acting2.html

Actingbiz
http://actingbiz.com

American Film Institute
http://www.afi.com

Children's Creative Theater
http://library.thinkquest.org/5291

Dream/Girl Magazine: The Arts Magazine for Girls
http://www.dgarts.com/content/movfilmcritic.htm

The Internet Movie Database
http://www.imdb.com

Music Notes
http://library.thinkquest.org/15413

Teacher's Guide: Academy Award Series
http://www.oscars.org/teachersguide